THE TH
GOLDEN

TO

WYE VALLEY
&
FOREST OF DEAN

Main Text: Mabel Beech

Series Editor: John Pemberthy

THORNHILL PRESS
Publishers

First Published in 1994 by Thornhill Press Ltd, Gloucestershire.
© Series and concept Thornhill Press Ltd, 1994
© Main text Mabel Beech 1994.

ISBN 0 946328 50 1

Printed in Great Britain by Hillman Printers (Frome) Ltd,
Frome, Somerset.

CONTENTS

Introduction

This guide to the Leadon Valley, Wye Valley, Severn Valley and Forest of Dean covers some of the most beautiful, interesting, and in the main, unexploited areas in this country. The beauty of the Wye Valley is well known and the much visited Symonds Yat is a greatly appreciated beauty spot. There are, however, other dimensions to this area as yet undiscovered, or little known. Plant and wild life abound in the woodlands which fringe the river on its journey through some of the most glorious countryside and which holds an open invitation at all times of the year to those who would explore.

Charming cottages cling to the steep hillsides and look down upon the Wye as it meanders through the fields and woodlands. Small villages cluster beside the river and invite all to stop for a while and savour the beauty and the history in which they are wrapped.

The west side of the Severn Valley is a place rich in the delights which abound in this fertile area. Life close to the tidal, navigable waters of the river, has been much involved with the business of wresting a living from the often unpredictable waters. Salmon fishing is an established business. For many years the river was a very important means of transport and shipping still uses the broad back of the Severn's waters.

The rich soil of this valley has been used for agricultural purposes since before the Romans came up to this present day.

From Westbury on Severn, where a wide sweep of the river is held in the embrace of the Garden Cliff, and the church stands apart from its tower, to Beachley where Offa's Dyke ends and Wye meets Severn, there are many traces of past history.

The Forest of Dean - the high wooded country rising between the two rivers, Wye and Severn, is one of the oldest forests in this country. A primeval forest well known to the great Norman kings. William the Conqueror came to Gloucester where he held his Christmas court and hunted in his Forest of Dean which, at that time, was rather more extensive in that it stretched to the very edge of Gloucester itself.

Because it was favoured by kings and noblemen as a hunting ground, the Forest of Dean became a royal forest. The tranquility of the forest land is no longer disturbed by the chase but deer still wander in the depths of the woodlands.

Over the years the boundary of the Forest of Dean has changed many times. The Speech House has always stood in the very heart and centre of the forest. The Forest Enterprise threshold signs indicate the extent of the ancient and recognised Forest of Dean. It is a place of history, for the past is woven inextricably into the area of the forest and its environs. The present has been very effectively created by what has gone before and the influences of the past can never be forgotten for they are the very fabric of the places of interest.

With a strange insularity of people and place brought about by its position between the two rivers, it is only in more recent years that the isolation and individuality of the Forest of Dean has been breached. This came about with the loss of the mining industry, which had been a major industrial feature in the Dean since time immemorial, and the building of the Severn Bridge which made it a much more accessible place. Even though that which set the forest apart, making it a little bit of Britain caught between England and Wales and having no wish to belong to either place, has gone, the traditions and privileges, some of which are unique, are still maintained and often jealously guarded.

The Leadon Valley does not have such an impressive waterway as Wye or Severn but its small river has brought richness and fecundity to the countryside which surrounds it.

The area of the Leadon is so fertile and productive that it could well be known as "The Garden of Gloucestershire". In the months of springtime it is carpeted by the gold of daffodils and crowned with the blossoms of countless fruit trees. Period cottages nestle in unexpected places and villages exude the timelessness of an area which has for so long been a place where man has chosen to spend his life in the peace and solitude of beautiful countryside.

Poets of fame, and other writers, have found inspiration and contentment in this place of orchards and woodland.

Unspoilt, uncommercialised and relatively unknown the valley of the Leadon is typically English. There could be no better setting for the home of Dick Whittington, who originated from these parts, than the small settlement dreaming beside the lazy waters of the River Leadon.

All these places have been linked by the towns which are the centres of commerce for the districts in which they stand. Individual characters have contributed to the cultural and historical life of the area. Some have left such an imprint on the places they have touched that they can never be forgotten.

Although this book has been written primarily as a guide, it will be of great value to anyone seeking to know more about the area of the Leadon Valley, Wye Valley, Severn Valley and the Forest of Dean.

Mabel Beech
1994.

HOW TO USE THIS GUIDE

The text has been written in such a way that it can be enjoyably read straight through by the armchair reader. The routes through the area can be followed in part or whole, depending on the time available, or reference can be made directly to the places of particular interest to the reader.

Each section has been devised for the convenience of those wishing to cover the entire area in a structured way and taking into account the need to follow the course of the major rivers to the east or west where there are no bridges. It is, however, perfectly possible to devise different routes by reference to the maps at the start of each section and by cross referencing the material within the sections.

Due to the need to find a route that takes the reader through the Forest of Dean without constantly back tracking, from St Briavels there are two alternative routes which need not be followed strictly if recourse is made to the map for the section. Both routes make excellent outings and, if time allows, provide the best method of seeing everything without unnecessary driving.

It is highly recommended that readers visit one of the Tourist Information Offices in the area where free pamphlets are available on facilities for tourists. A listing of the major tourist sites is given at the end of this book. Readers should telephone for details of opening times and entrance prices where applicable.

ROSS - LEADON VALLEY

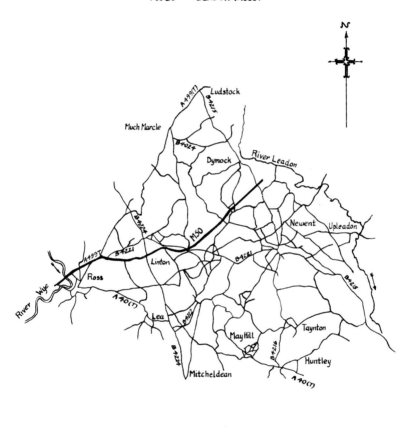

Scale ½" to 1 mile   Drawn by G.L.Clissold.

Newent
and the
Leadon Valley

N E W E N T
Gloucester - 10
Ross - 9
Hereford - 13
Office of Tourism - Library, High Street
Early Closing - Wed. (some shops)
Market Day - Friday
Library - High Street

See Gazetteer for leisure and recreational facilities

of Dean has always been an agricultural area.

The name of Newent was derived from a new inn (according to Leland), built to accomodate travellers when the route to Wales was first opened this way.

Newent was a small market town. It lies off the B4215 road which comes from the directions of Gloucester and Ross.

Although it is not situated on any major route, Newent is a bustling small town with several villages, hamlets and farms in the locality, of which it is the commercial centre.

Although it is part of the administrative area of the Forest of Dean, Newent has only one thing noticeably in common with that district, and that is mining. At one time Newent had coal and iron mines, but unlike the Forest

Market Hall, Newent.

Evidence has been found of much earlier settlers in this area. Bronze Age weapons have been discovered, and several caches of

Roman coins have been unearthed.

The old **Market Hall** is one of Newent's greatest treasures. It stands in the centre of the town raised on sixteen oak pillars. It is said to be Elizabethan. The builder of the Market House was a Dutchman who signed his work with the ball and flute carvings on the under beams.

The lovely black and white **Market House** was restored in 1864 by Richard Foley-Onslow who was then the Lord of the Manor of Newent. In 1913 the Market House was sold by the Onslow family. It was presented to the Town Council by Henry Bruton. The building was again restored in 1991, and has been much renovated over the years. Newent's other building of note is the church.

At the time of the Conquest the **Manor of Newent** was granted to the Earl of Hereford and given to the Benedictine monks at the Abbey of Cormeilles in Normandy. They founded a priory at Newent. The priory at Chepstow was also founded by the same order and

NEWENT

1 Market Square & House.
2 Museum.
3 St Mary's Church.
4 Library (Tourist Information Centre.)

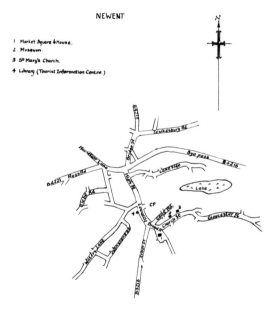

100 200 300 400 yds

Drawn by G.L.Clissold 1994

Street map of Newent

from the same French Abbey. The Manor of Newent was taken over by Edward III and Henry IV and was eventually taken by the Crown at the time of the Reformation.

It was claimed that, during the Reformation, the lead was taken from the church roof. After a very heavy fall of snow on January 18th 1673 the nave was destroyed. The restoration work was carried out by a carpenter from Newent, Edward Taylor, who had worked in London under Wren. The masons were Francis Jones and James Hill from Hasfield and Cheltenham.

It is recorded that Charles II made a grant of sufficient oak from the Forest of Dean to carry out the re-roofing work. The roof was made with a single span which proved to be most effective. The work was completed in 1680. Edward Taylor, the man who designed the roof replacement and carried out this great task, is buried in the graveyard of Newent church.

The church of St. Mary is large, with a tall spire some 153 feet high. It has a shaft of an early cross, probably 9th century, certainly pre-Norman. There are several items of interest in the church including the east window in the chancel and the Lady Chapel.

There are some timber framed houses in Newent, now much renovated which, like the Market House, date from Elizabethan times. The Tan House in Culver Street dates from about the end of the 17th century.

The George Hotel, the oldest inn in Newent, was once a coaching inn. It was also the place from which the Royal Mail coaches departed. There are several things of great interest in and around Newent.

The Shambles

The Shambles Museum is tucked away behind the houses of Church Street. It is a museum of life as it was in Victorian times. There is an exact reproduction of a home, reflecting the life style of the people who would have lived in it - the fictional Mrs and Mr Wells. Shops of that day and age undoubtedly flourished in the Newent of that period. There is a gift shop; it is possible to have light lunches in the licensed restaurant, and also coffee and tea.

The Cowdy Glass Workshop can be found in Culver Street in Newent. Here visits are allowed for a small fee. Craftsmen can be seen at work blowing and fashioning glass into various items. The work with glass includes such things as engraving. It is possible to look around the shop and gallery without going into the workshops, and items can be bought there.

Newent has two vineyards. One is at the Oxenhall about 1.7 miles from Newent leading off the B4221 from Woodyard. This is the **St. Anne Vineyard**. This vineyard went into production in 1984 and the 'cellar' includes some country wines made from fruits such as blackberry, redcurrant and other more exotic fruits. The vineyard also produces traditional English wines made from grapes from their locally grown vines.

The Three Choirs vineyard is one and a half miles outside Newent on the B4215 Dymock-Leominster road. This vineyard has very effectively revived the tradition of producing excellent English wines. The Romans first introduced vines and wines to this country, and The Three Choirs vineyard has more than recaptured this worthy tradition. Their products have attracted much acclaim, with many national and international awards have been won for the excellence of the wines produced here.

The name 'Three Choirs', was given because the vineyards are situated almost in the centre of the Hereford, Gloucester and Worcester areas where, in the cathedrals of these three cities, the prestigious music festival of that name is celebrated each year.

The first vintage came from the Three Choirs vineyard in 1975. Since that time its success has been so rapid that today it is one of the six largest vineyards in this country.

The Three Choirs vineyard welcomes visitors. Anyone can call during opening hours to buy from the Pantry. Parking is free, and facilities for disabled and toilets are provided. Conducted tours are offered, but prior notice is needed particularly for parties. Wine tastings are free. The vineyard has an excellent restaurant which provides teas and lunches and can also cater for weddings, conferences etc.

Newent is a good centre from which to explore the surrounding area. It has many attractions, and this border country between Gloucestershire and Herefordshire is full of interest and beauty. It is much enhanced by the fact that it has not yet been 'discovered' and so has not suffered from over exploitation.

The Vale of Leadon covers the area from Ledbury to the Isle of Alney where the Leadon joins the Severn. It passes through rich farm land - highly productive 'red soil'. The villages of the Leadon include **Pauntley, Kempley. Upleadon, Dymock and Taynton.**

The villages of the Leadon are all with in a five mile radius of Newent. The area used to be known as 'the daffodil belt' because in springtime this area was once golden with the wild 'Lenten Lily'. Sadly, many of the fields are now put to more utilitarian and productive use. The wild daffodils now only grow in profusion in the woodlands around Dymock. After the daffodils, the orchards are filled with the glory of the fruit trees in blossom. If the Leadon Valley blooms in the springtime then in the autumn it is fruitful. There is a plum called the Dymock plum which is very good for making jam.

This is a beautiful bit of the countryside where Gloucestershire gently drifts into Herefordshire. Thankfully the Leadon Valley has never been over exploited even though it has all the ingredients of a place well worth visiting.

From Newent it is just three miles to Pauntley. All the villages are well signposted. The journey from Newent to Pauntley is truly rural. Pauntley itself is in an idyllic setting. The church is at the main entrance gate to Pauntley Court. Pauntley is famous for the fact that this was the home of the legendary **Dick Whittington**. It was from this tiny place that he set out with his faithful cat on his fateful journey to London. His first stop, so we are to believe, was at Westgate Street in Gloucester.

The church stands on a swell in the meadow land and looks out over the lazily flowing river Leadon. It is a small church built in Norman times and dedicated to St. John.

The Whittingtons lived at **Pauntley Court** and the arms of that family are incorporated into one of the windows of the church. Today there is some interest being shown in the buildings which comprise the present day Pauntley Court which has been re-built since the days of Dick Whittington. It is thought that one of the old buildings around the

Court could be the 'Manor House' home of the Whittingtons. Dick Whittington was born in 1358 and went to be an apprentice in London - the rest is well known.

It is just four miles from Pauntley to Dymock - a place which once acquired some measure of fame for a very unusual reason. For most local people Dymock was known for the fact that it is well established in the golden belt of daffodils which, in their season, once spread much colour and joy to the countryside tired from the long months of winter. Could it be this that brought several aspiring and established poets to make their homes here in the years prior to the First World War ?

John Frost came here. He was to be, according to the local press, 'America's unofficial Poet Laureate'. Frost lived with his family at 'Little Iddens', a 17th century cottage.

Lascelles Abercrombie came here to live in 1911. He lived in a typical country cottage in Ryton. It was known that his writings were inspired by the place - such as:

'From Marcle Way
From Dymock, Kempley,
Newent, Bromsberrow,
Redmarley, all the
Meadowland daffodils seem
Running in golden tides to
Ryton Firs

Wilfred Gibson, John Drinkwater and **Rupert Brooke** were all living in or around Dymock. With Lascelles Abercrombie they joined together to produce a magazine to promote poetry. The magazine was called 'New Numbers'. The onset of the First World War was to dash any hopes of success they had with this venture. The gathering was to be known as the **'Dymock Poets'**, and although their stay in this beautiful part of the country did not last for many years it was to make a lasting impression on the locality.

The village of Dymock is surrounded by the **Dymock Woods** which still take on the golden glow of the daffodils in the springtime. The Dymock Woods of Gloucestershire and Herefordshire come under the care of Forest Enterprise. The woods are a mixed growth of trees with the sessile oak growing very vigorously on the soil of this area. Woodland management is carried out to promote conservation and to encourage interesting bird life and butterflies. About twenty per cent of the woodlands are sites of special scientific interest (S.S.S.I's). There are pursuits which should appeal to a large number of people. For walkers there are five colour way-marked routes with distances varying between one mile and $3^1/2$ miles. The leaflets on these particular walks can be obtained from the Shaw Common office of Forest Enterprise (tel:

Gorsley 235). There are other walks with leaflets published by the Windcross Public Paths Project. These are available through Tourist Information Centres. Picnic sites have been made at strategic places. In Queen's Wood there is a man-made lake which attracts a deal of wildlife, duck and wildfowl. Fishing permits can be obtained from the local Forest Enterprise office at Shaw Common. Permits for horseriders are also available from the same office.

The different areas of the Dymock Woods have some truly fascinating names, such as 'Colonel's Grove', 'Daw's Coppice', and 'Daubies Wood' each offering its own particular woodland interest. Dymock was a settlement before the Romans came and was a place of some importance during the Roman occupation. It was similarly important during Saxon times and when William the Conqueror compiled the Domesday Book it was quite a large royal Manor. There was considerably more woodland at Dymock then. Today the Dymock Woods cover some 2,000 acres.

The village of Dymock is a lively and very community minded place. It has some attractive houses. One house of particular interest is the 'White House' (which is actually red). It stands across Wintour's Green on the opposite side of the B4215 Leominster road to the church. This was the house where John Kyrle, the famous 'Man of Ross', was born in 1637.

The Church dedicated to **St. Mary the Virgin** is built of rose tinted stone. In the large churchyard there is an avenue of lime trees. These mark the course of the Roman road which once traversed this place.

Kempley is one of the Leadon valley villages which has built itself something of a reputation for its springtime 'daffodil teas' which are now an established tradition and annually raise funds for Kempley Church. There is also a 'Daffodil Sunday' around Easter time. The village of Kempley is situated some two miles to the south west of Dymock in the direction of Ross on Wye.

The place is set amongst the delightful countryside and has two churches. The smaller, **St. Mary's Church**, built in the twelfth century, was possibly built here because it was on a trackway between the two important cities of Hereford and Gloucester.

William the Conqueror gave Kempley to the De Lacy family. The fact is echoed in that a member of that family is depicted as a character in some wonderful mural paintings which have been discovered in this ancient church. They are on the chancel wall and the vault. These paintings, many of them now indistinct, are thought to be the most important paintings of their kind in this country. It is supposed that most of the mural paintings are as old as the chancel, itself dating from about 1110.

Perhaps the most impressive of these murals is the 'Glorification of the Redeemer' which takes up the whole centre of the low barrel vault of the chancel.

This church is worth visiting if only to see these old paintings which were covered with whitewash for hundreds of years. They were discovered in 1872 and varnished over. In 1955 they were expertly cleaned. Restoration of these paintings was extensive and extremely well done.

The church is a squat sort of building. Best described as rather quaint; it seems to huddle into the low land on which it stands.

The tower of the church was probably built as some sort of refuge or fortification agains Welsh incursions. It has no windows, just a few arrow slits. The tower was added at the end of the 13th century.

The other Kempley church, that of **St. Edward**, was built by Earl Beauchamp in 1903 about a mile away from the Norman church on much higher ground. From this church there is a magnificent view of the Malvern Hills.

Upleadon is beyond Newent in the direction of Corse Lawn and Hartpury. It is a pleasant place in the quiet Leadon valley. It has one very prominent landmark **'Eden's Hill'** which provides a very good viewpoint from which the Severn valley can be clearly seen.

The church stands a little apart from the village. There is a sculptured tympanum over the ancient Norman door.

From Upleadon follow the road in the direction of **Highleadon** where the B4215 is taken in the direction of **Tibberton**. This is the village which is a close neighbour of **Taynton.**

Taynton - this truly rural village is best known for its connections with the activities of the Civil War in this locality. It was the scene of many skirmishes during that unhappy period in our country's history.

At that time the ancient church at Taynton, dedicated to **St. Lawrence**, was in a bad state of disrepair. It was due to be thoroughly renovated. In 1643, as a direct result of a Civil War incident, it was burnt to the ground.

A new church was built, by order of Parliament, about 1648. Thomas Pury M.P. for Gloucester, a supporter of Massey, was largely responsible for the building of the church on its present site.

May Hill

Taynton village had a re-enactment of the happenings of the Civil War in 1993. It was held at Taynton House and recounted the battle which took place there between the opposing forces of the Round heads and Cavaliers. Its activities came to a climax with the recalling of the burning of the church. It was a real village community venture with nearly everyone playing a part in this exciting taste of Taynton's past history.

Taynton House is one of the most interesting buildings in this area. It is a sixteenth century building which has, over the years, had alterations and additions to its original construction but still maintains a deal of its original charm.

The Grove, another Taynton house of note, was at the time of the Civil War the home of Thomas Pury M.P. for Gloucester. His coat of arms is on the fireback in one of the rooms.

Hown Hall is another building of some consequence. A nice farmhouse which dates from the eighteenth century, it rests in the shadow of May Hill.

May Hill is one of the best known and prominent landmarks in the whole of Gloucestershire. Rising from behind the village of Huntley it is a thousand feet above sea level. What makes May Hill so distinctive is that it has a crown of trees set upon its rounded summit.

There are several ways to approach May Hill. From Taynton it is best to ignore the road sign which says 'Newent' B4216 and take the next direction, at the next road junction, to 'May Hill'.

From whichever direction May Hill is approached, the ascent to the summit has to be made on foot. From this suggested direction the climb is possibly not as steep as it would be from any other point. If May Hill can be seen from many places, its summit commands a view which is extensive.

There are many stories and legends about May Hill. Today, certain people still wait on May Hill's top to greet the first day of May. The popular story is that the crown of trees on top of May Hill was planted to mark the jubilee of Queen Victoria. However, in 'The Diary of a Cotswold Parson', the Reverend F.E. Witts, writing about the happenings of August 26th 1820, has this to say about his approach to the Hill -

"... In front, May Hill, a conspicuous round topped hill distinguished by a plantation on the summit"

May Hill is now looked after by the National Trust. Reflecting on the crown of trees at the summit, it was mentioned by John Masefield in his writing "The Everlasting Mercy".

May Hill

Above the plains of Gloucester
She lifts her rounded head,
Looks over field and forest
Where countryside is spread.
Looks to the distant Cotswolds,
Wrapped in a misty haze,
She stands above the busy world

And man's so hurried ways.
Yet he has paid her homage
With ancient mystic rite
Has waited on her hilltop
To greet the sun's first light.
Has made her ring with merry song,
Has touched with dancing feet.
And nowhere can a place afford
A view that is so sweet.
Countless are the travellers,
Who through the many years,
Have seen her rising glory
With thankfulness - and tears.
Proudly - yes - and rightly.
She wears a crown of green.
For of all the hills in Gloucestershire
MAY she is the Queen.

MB

Leaving May Hill it is possible to join the B4216 on an unclassified road from near the 'Glasshouse' at May Hill. Before reaching Newent, just off this road is -

The National Birds of Prey Centre
This place plays a major role in the conservation and preservation of many species of birds of prey which are at risk of extinction. Captive breeding is carried out here and this Centre has national fame. It was founded in 1967 as a Falconry Centre by Philip Glasier, who was renowned for his work with birds of prey, and falcons in particular. He wrote several books amongst which were 'As the Falcon Her Bells' and the autobiographical 'A Hawk in the Hand' as well as his definitive work 'Falconry and Hawking'.

The Centre was taken over by Philip Glasier's daughter Jemima

Parry-Jones. Under her direction the centre has become 'The National Birds of Prey Centre' and is recognised as the largest private collection of birds of prey in Europe. Jemima Parry-Jones is well known for television appearances and the demonstrations with the birds which she gives at many major events. She also writes about her work with, and interest in, birds of prey, as her book 'Falconry' illustrates.

There are flying displays given at the centre at specified times during opening hours. The centre provides endless interest to everyone. There are adequate parking facilities, a book and country gift shop, refreshments, a picnic area and a children's play area. Disabled visitors are welcomed.

From the National Birds of Prey Centre it is just a short distance to Newent. From Newent take the B4221 through Kilcot and Gorsley to the M50 which leads to Ross on Wye.

ROSS – MONMOUTH

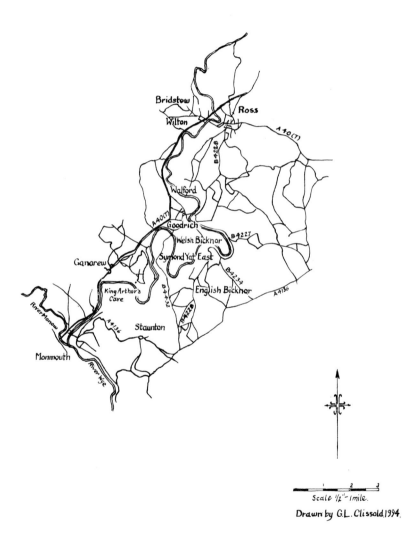

Scale ½" – 1 mile.

Drawn by G.L. Clissold 1994.

Ross on Wye
to
Monmouth

R O S S   O N   W Y E

Gloucester - 17 miles
Hereford - 15 miles
Monmouth - 11 miles
Market Days - Thursday
  and Saturday; Friday
  (livestock)
Office of Tourism - 20 Broad
  Street.
Coach Depot - Homs Road.

See Gazetteer for leisure and
recreational facilities

The area East of the Wye.

Ross on Wye is an extremely pleasant small market town. Although there has been extensive development in around this town, it is in no way obtrusive or out of keeping with the character of the place.

Ross has one of the oldest weather observations in this country. Weather messages from Ross are relayed to every weather bureau in Europe each day.

Market Place, Ross

ROSS ON WYE

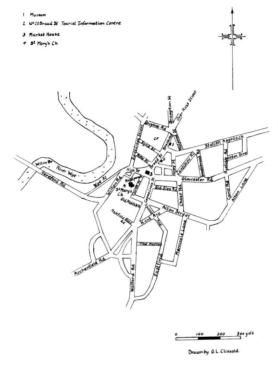

1 Museum
2 N°20 Broad St Tourist Information Centre
3 Market House
4 St Mary's Ch

Drawn by G.L.Clissold.

Street map of Ross

The focal point of the town is the old **Market Hall**. This was built in the reign of Charles II. It is an impressive building standing in a commanding position at the top of the main street virtually surrounded by the, often busy, thoroughfare. It is also the venue for the twice weekly street markets.

The Market Hall is overlooked, from the opposite side of the street at its rear, by the black and white buildings, which were once home of John Kyrle **'The Man of Ross'**. This building is now two shops.

One is occupied by the Ross Gazette, the local weekly newspaper, the other is a Chemist's shop. Over the one building is a sign which indicates it was the house of the 'Man of Ross; and, over the Chemist's shop is a medallion of the 'Man of Ross'.

Born in nearby Dymock in 1637 John Kyrle was the son of the M.P. for Leominster. After being educated at Oxford, John Kyrle made his home, for the rest of his natural life, in Ross. He was a magistrate but rarely took his seat on the bench. He was also, in 1683, the High Sheriff of Herefordshire. He died, in 1724, at the age of 87. John Kyrle was one of the most renowned men Ross has ever known. He never married. He earned his fame by his kindness and generosity to Ross and the people of that place.

History tells us what a munificent benefactor John Kyrle was. His charity to others was unbounded. What money he had, he spent helping those in need.

Amongst the many benefits he bestowed on the people of Ross was the construction of the raised roadway from Wilton into the town to help those who had cause to use that road in times of flood. He also brought the water supply to Ross, and gained access to the Prospect for the people of the place. John Kyrle was immortalised by the poet Alexander Pope (1688-1744) who, even though he did not know John Kyrle, had heard of his good works and wrote, extolling the virtues of the man in verse. Part of that poem reads as follows :-

Beyond the market place o'erspread
The Man of Ross divides the weekly bread;
He feeds yon almshouse, neat but void of state,
Where age and want sit smiling at the gate;
Him portion'd maids, apprentic'd orphans bless,
The young who labour, and the old who rest.
Is any sick ? The Man of Ross relieves
Prescribes, attends, the medicine make and gives.....

In 1794 Coleridge stayed at the King's Arms. He paid his personal tribute, to John Kyrle, in verse.

Nobler than kings or king-polluted Lords,
Here dwelt then man of Ross.

In the year 1924 a clock was put in the Church tower to mark the bi-centenary of John Kyrle's death.

The area around the parish church of **St. Mary** is one of the most pleasant in this lovely little town. For here, the Prospect which are public gardens, can be visited. From this very descriptively named place, which invites all who visit it to sit and pause a while, there are lovely views over the sweep of the river Wye which touches Ross at this point.

Strangely Ross is approached from the Gloucestershire side on level roads. From this, the **Wilton Bridge** direction, this part of Ross stands on sand stone cliffs rising above the river. It gives it an enviable vantage point.

In the vicinity of the church can be found the bowling green, tennis courts and putting green which provide leisure activities for many people. It is known as **'Old Maid's Walk,'**

The parish church of St. Mary is an impressive building. Standing on high ground it dominates the town and can be seen clearly as a distinctive landmark from the A40 and A449 which links the M5 with South Wales. The church dates from the thirteenth century but has obviously had several major renovations in the intervening years. As recently as 1911 the tower was restored other changes have been since that date.

In the year 1637, Ross was ravaged by the Plague. It swept through the town. The pestilence was widespread. No family seemed to escape. There is, in the churchyard near the entrance from **Church Street**, a large stone cross. This marks the burial of 315 victims of the Plague outbreak in the town of Ross.

Also in the church, are several monuments commemorating the **Rudhall family**. The monument to William Rudhall, who died in 1651 and was a Colonel and a Commander of the local Royalist troop during the Civil War, is portrayed in Roman armour atop a pedestal.

Near the church there is a memorial to another benefactor of Ross. His name was **Walter Scott**. This son of a Ross carpenter left his home to seek fame and fortune in London. This he found. When he returned to Ross, late in his life, Walter Scott found his old school in a serious state of disrepair. When he died in 1786 Walter Scott left the fortune he

had accrued in his lifetime for the re-establishment of the Blue Coat Charity School in Ross. It was named after him and was known as 'The Walter Scott' school. This school closed about 1928 and today the money from the endowment is used to aid students seeking further education.

In Church Street, which rises rapidly past the north-east boundary wall of the church, can be found some lovely old almshouses. These houses still maintain their Tudor frontage and were built for the town by the Rudhall family in the seventeenth century. There are also old almshouses in **Copse Cross Street.**

The main thoroughfare is now the **Gloucester Road** but previously it was the narrow street known as the Old Gloucester Road. When **George IV** was travelling through Ross in 1821 on his way from Fishguard, he was held up in this narrow street by an unattended cart. He was very angry about this delay and had to wait whilst the offending cart owner was found. On arriving in London the King sent a message to Ross saying that if the road through the town was not improved then they would lose their status on the mail route. Consequently the road we know today was made.

The Old Gloucester Road ran in front of the **Royal Hotel**. This was a most prestigious hotel in that

The Royal, Ross

it was one of the first luxury hotels in the South West of England. It now belongs to the Trusthouse Forte group. **Charles Dickens** and his biographer, John Forster, stayed at the Royal Hotel in 1867 and much enjoyed the wonderful views over the Wye. There is now a 'Dicken's Room' at the hotel where visitors can enjoy the pleasures of the Royal Hotel and its superb situation. Many important people came to stay at the Royal Hotel in the nineteenth century. They included Royalty since **Queen Victoria** and the young princess who was to become Queen Mary honoured the hotel and the town with a visit.

Just beside the Royal Hotel, and in the shadow of the church, can be found the **Theatre of Ross**. This small theatre, built on the site of the old fire station and aptly called **The Phoenix**, is a great asset to the town. It is well supported for all its excellent productions.

One of the most remarkable men to have had very close connections with Ross must be **Sir Frederick Burrows**. He was born at **Bollow**, near Westbury on Severn, and worked as a checker on the railways in that area. With his family he lived at a place called **Northwood Green**. He went to do service in the first world war where he was Company Sergeant Major in the

Grenadier Guards. On his return from the army Frederick Burrows returned to his work on the railways. In 1923 the Burrows family moved to Ross where, Frederick Burrows worked as a porter at Ross, and then, as a checker, at nearby **Backney Halt**. He became the secretary of his local branch of the National Union of Railwaymen. In 1938 he was elected to the union's national executive. During the very difficult years of the War he served as National President. His undoubted talents were noticed by the Prime Minister of the day, **Winston Churchill**, and Frederick Burrows was appointed to serve on a Commission to constitutional reform in Ceylon.

Later, in 1945, Prime Minister Attlee appointed Frederick Burrows to be Governor General of Bengal. This was a most important post. He became Grand Commander of the Order of the Indian Empire.

In 1946 Frederick Burrows was knighted. He also became Knight Commander of the Order of the Star of India. He was to be the last British Governor of Bengal. He earned great respect for the way in which he conducted himself and carried out his duties whilst he was in high office. On his return to Ross, Sir Frederick Burrows, was to become **High Sheriff of Herefordshire.** Chairman of the Ross Magistrates. A local director of Lloyds Bank. The last Chairman

of the Agriculture Land Commission and a member of the Royal Commission on Marriage and Divorce. He was also Chairman of the Wye River Authority. When Sir Frederick Burrows died in 1973 the Queen was represented at his funeral. Ross on Wye has much to offer. Not only does it enjoy a temperate climate but it can offer a variety of leisure activities, clubs and organisations to suit all types of tastes. It also has excellent shopping facilities.

In Old Gloucester Road is the candle-maker's shop and in **Kyrle Street** the award-winning **Button Museum.** Beneath a covered way in **Brookend Street** it is possible to take a step back in time into the **'Lost Street Museum'**. It features shops and a pub dating from 1885 to 1935. It is a place of great fascination.

There are many old buildings in Ross which have been preserved. **The Rosswyn Hotel** is one such place. It is in the, slightly bent, **Copse Cross Street** not far from the market place. This building dates from the fifteenth century and reflects the charm and character of a well loved old place. It has an Elizabethan fireplace in one of the rooms.

The area around the A45 which leads out of Ross in the direction of Hereford drops from the high area of the town down to the river. To the left of the road is the

Ross Sports Club. On the right is a very pleasant area much enjoyed by many people. It is a favourite place for walks and picnics for here the river flows through public land. The nearby 'Anchor Inn' often provides some sort of outdoor entertainment, such as a local brass or silver band playing, particularly on Sunday evenings in the summer months. **The Ross Rowing Club** also operates from this area.

About two miles on the other side of Ross, on the A40, is the small village of **Weston Under Penyard.** At the **Weston Cross Inn**, to the left, is an unclassified road which leads to **Rudhall**, and **Bollitree**. At Rudhall is the House where once lived the famous **Rudhall family** who made such an impression on the life and history of nearby Ross. At Bollitree are the remains of the famous Roman Ariconium.

Ariconium

This place was, in Roman times, a very important industrial centre. Here was smelted the iron that came from the Forest of Dean. Even though for the casual observer there is little to be seen at this Ariconium site, for the archaeologist it has provided a virtual treasure trove of artefacts from that Roman time.

In the years, after the Romans left our shores, this site became a forgotten place even though there was much speculation about the important Roman Ariconium and where it could be. For fourteen hundred years it lay beneath the meadowland in this quiet place virtually undisturbed. Legend says that stone was taken from Ariconium in Saxon times to build dwellings at the place now known as **Brookend** in Ross. In the late years of the eighteenth century the farmer who, at that time owned **Bollitree Farm**, found some evidence of something of interest beneath his land. Subsequent excavations revealed that this was indeed the site of the great Roman industrial centre which had been lost for so many years. It covered a large area and has been a source of much interest ever since. Excavations have revealed smelting furnaces, ironworks and forges and extensive debris from these activities. Roman coins and other items have, from time to time, been discovered here, as well as a great deal of pottery.

It was also found that many roads, from Roman times, led to Ariconium. One of these was the **Dean Road** which passes through the Forest of Dean from near Lydney. Making its way to Ariconium the Dean Road passes through the Forest of Dean villages of **Soudley, Littledean, Mitcheldean** and in Herefordshire, the **Lea village**.

Leaving Weston under Penyard to return to Ross, on the left can be seen the **Chase Hill**. This is the highest point in this area and rises to a height of some 650 ft. Chase Hill has been of some archaeological interest. Neolithic flint artefacts have been found there and its present form is that of the pre-Roman Age.

From Ross the B4228 leads towards the village of Walford. About two miles from Ross just before reaching the village, near the church, is a road, on the right, leading to a very interesting house.

The Hillcourt House

The Mansion House, which dates from the reign of William and Mary, is approached through splendid iron gates and at the end of a well distanced straight drive the house is most impressive.

The building of this superb Mansion house was instigated, by a certain Richard Clarke, in 1698. It remained in the possession of that family until the death of Jane Clarke in 1806.

In 1851 the Hillcourt House became the home of Captain Kingsmill Evans. Then it passed to Kingsmill Manley-Power. His great-grandson, Mr Manley Power, was the last Lord of the Manor of Ross on Wye. The present owners of the property do not allow access to members of the public.

Walford

This small riverside village strong community spirit. The village of Walford had a generous benefactor, for it benefitted greatly, under the will of a son of the place. His name was **Robert Pashley**. He was the son of a solicitor. Robert Pashley was born, and lived all his life, in the village of Walford. He loved the River Wye at that spot. He served in the 1914/18 War. Having been well educated he was, several times, offered a commission which he refused saying he preferred to spend his time with the ordinary men of the army. Robert Pashley returned to Walford and to his life centred around the river. He had boats and a ghillie. It was claimed that he caught more salmon on that stretch of river than any other man. In fifty years he caught 10,237 salmon. He was known as 'The Wizard of the Wye'. He married and served his village as Chairman of the Managers of the School and was also an alderman.

When Robert Pashley died he left the bulk of his considerable wealth for setting up a Trust Fund for Walford School. The purpose of the Fund was to pay for an annual educational outing for the children and to help children from the school who went to the universities, further education or into apprenticeships. A fine recreation ground was also bought for the School. From public subscriptions the 'Robert Pashley'

Hall, was built for the whole community. The Hall is a very fitting memorial to a son of Walford to whom the village, and its particular bit of the River Wye, meant so very much.

Walford Parish Church is dedicated to **St. Michael and All Angels** and was, until 1887, known as the Church of St. Leonard. This church has ancient origins and, possibly, there was a church on this site before Norman times. The Nave of the present church dates from about 1100. The north aisle was added in the middle years of the thirteenth century, and, about 1430 there were other major additions. The font dates from the fifteenth century. Thomas Dudley Fosbrooke, a noted historian and antiquarian, was the incumbent here at Walford between 1800 and 1842. There is a memorial tablet to him in the chancel. A funerary helm of Lieutenant-Colonel Kyrle hangs over the chancel arch. Outside the church there is a pointed stone. This is an ancient parish boundary marker.

From Walford it is a short distance to the **Kerne Bridge**. This bridge,

The Kerne Bridge

which crosses the Wye, was built in 1826 and for many years was a toll bridge with a resident toll keeper.

On a hilltop at the other side of the river, the considerable ruins of Goodrich Castle can be seen etched against the skyline.

At this point the River Wye begins its journey through some of the tree clad hills which contribute so much to its beauty. Around this area is the **Coppet Hill** and on the east side are the wooded heights which fringe the Forest of Dean.

Bishopswood

Here can be seen the **Lodge Grove Brook.** It was alongside this waterway that, in the 1590s, the second Earl of Essex established two of the first blast furnaces in the Forest of Dean. Near the **Bishopswood Church**, in 1895, a hoard of 17,000 fourth century, Roman coins were discovered.

It was around Bishopswood, and the small Forest village of Ruardean, that **Captain Mayne Reid** based his novel 'No Quarter'. This work, of fiction, told of exciting happenings, in that area during

Lydbrook Viaduct

the troublous years of the Civil War. Whilst writing this book Captain Mayne Reid lived just

outside Ross-on-Wye. The book is now a collector's item.

The B4228 leads on to Lydbrook. Just before reaching that place there is a turning to the left, which leads up the Vention Lane. It is an extremely steep and restricted road. Halfway up this turning can be found the '**Royal Spring Inn'.** Adjacent to the public house, can be seen, some very well restored lime-kilns. This is a pleasant 'off the beaten track' hostelry which has much to offer visitors.

Lydbrook

This **Forest of Dean village** meanders down through a deep valley to be halted by the flow of the **River Wye.** On a north-east slope of the valley, in the centre of the upper part of the village, is the parish church dedicated to **The Holy Jesus**. It was consecrated in 1851.

On the opposite side of the road to the church is the village recreation ground. This is evidence of the stoic nature and spirit of the men of Lydbrook. For many years this area of Lydbrook was dominated by the Blue Mound. This was about 16,000 tons of slag from a mine. It was an eyesore and a blot on the landscape so the men of Lydbrook, of all ages, set about the mammoth task of removing the slag heap. They moved as much as 400 tons in a single day. It was very much a village effort. Young and old worked together and completed their task. In 1934, the then **Duke of Kent**, came down to Lydbrook to lay the first stone in the feature wall which was built to surround the recreation ground that had been made from the old coal tip. Down through the valley the houses cling, seemingly precariously in some instances, to the side of the steep hills on either side. There is, in the lower part of Lydbrook, a brown and white timbered house. This was where **Sarah Siddons,** the famous actress lived when she was a girl. Her name was Kemble. Her first London appearance was not a success. Then in 1782, after her second appearance on the London stage, she was much acclaimed as an incomparable tragic actress. She was very beautiful. She was born in 1755, retired from the stage in 1812 and died in 1831.

The deep valley at the bottom of Lydbrook was once spanned by a **viaduct.** This was built specifically to take the minerals out of the Forest of Dean. It was a great engineering feat and was erected by a Welsh company.

The last passenger train to cross this viaduct, which was very much a feature of the place, was in 1952 when a trip left Lydbrook to visit the exhibition in London. The viaduct was taken down in 1965. Traces of the beautiful stonework which was part of the viaduct can still be seen.

The area around the bottom of Lydbrook, close to the River Wye, is very pleasing. Some of the houses, many of which are renovated and restored, climb up the steep sides of the hills upon which they are built, and command lovely views over the river and surrounding countryside.

Probert's Barns Lane is part of a cross-forest prehistoric route and also served a Roman period residence. At the bottom of this lane is **The Old Post Office** which was one of the earliest Rowland Hill 'Penny Post Offices' of around 1840.

Alongside the Wye is the **Courtfield Arms**. It takes its name from the house which can be seen on top of the hill on the opposite side of the river. That house is Courtfield, a place of much history.

Around the corner from Courtfield Arms, is the **Forge Hammer** public house. This name is evocative of past industries. The Forge Hammer stands beside the brook which runs through the valley along which the village of Lydbrook is scattered. It was this brook which powered the furnaces, and forges, which were once very much a part of Lydbrook. Beside the river at the bottom of Lydbrook there is a very well kept and nicely set out small riverside park. It is a pleasant spot to sit and watch the wild life on the waters of the river or to see canoeists shooting the rapids around a small island in the river. Motorists should continue from the bottom of Lydbrook on the B4228.

English Bicknor

This small place standing in typical English countryside has most ancient origins. The Dean Archaeological Group have confirmed that human habitation commenced here more than 6,000 years ago. Large quantities of prehistoric flint artefacts have been recorded from this whole area by that Group. There is an identified Roman settlement at the southern end of the village.

The church at English Bicknor is delightful. It epitomises everyone's concept of an English country church with its lych gate, beautifully kept churchyard, and small school standing within the precincts of the church. It is a real English village setting.

The walls of the church are built on the foundations of a **Norman Castle** of which the foundations are still to be seen. The church was begun in the thirteenth century and finished in the fifteenth century. The tombstones in the churchyard provide fascinating evidence of the age of the church. Just outside the church gates are the **Lucy Machens Almshouses**. These houses were originally built in memory of Lucy Machen for those of the village who needed them.

In more recent years the almhouses have been sold and converted into flats. The proceeds from the sale were put into a trust fund which is administered by Trustees and the income is distributed to the poor of the place.

Bicknor Court is one of the oldest houses in the village. It has medieval origins. It is still a commanding impressive building.

Eastbach Court was the home of the Machens. They were the most powerful family to live in Bicknor in more recent years. 'Squire Machen', so it is recalled by many older folk, expected the lads to doff their caps and the girls to curtsey to him in the village street. He also expected all in his employ to be present in church on Sunday - or to have an extremely good excuse for not being there.

The Machens were very important people in the life of the Forest of Dean. In 1805 Edward Machen succeeded his father in both offices as Deputy Surveyor and Deputy Gaveller of Dean. He held office for fifty years and was to be the longest serving Deputy Surveyor the Forest of Dean has ever had.

English Bicknor is a wonderful place for exploration. It stands high above the River Wye with the lovely **Rosemary Topping Hill** and Raven's Cliff. Nearby are the **Coldwell Rocks**, everything is complemented by the trees which grow upon the heights, and sweep down to the river valley below. It is a paradise for all lovers of nature.

In the valley below the walker's trail continues along a disused **railway line**. This line once carried railborne traffic from Ross on Wye to Monmouth and Chepstow. This line, which opened in 1873, closed in 1959 under the Beeching axe. This disused railway track follows the route of the river to Monmouth, except where the tunnel used to run beneath the cliffs of Symond's Yat rock. The beauty of this area is almost indescribable.

From English Bicknor the B4228 leads through farmland to Christchurch. This is where the Forestry Commission, locally Forest Enterprise, have some of their camping sites with various facilities. All are in pleasant woodland country and extremely well maintained and organised by Forest Enterprise staff.

This village, spreading out from the crossroads, is within the forest proper. The church, which stands near the crossroads, has the distinction of being the very first church to have been built within the forest as defined by the ancient boundaries. It was built through the efforts of the Reverend Proctor, who was the incumbent at Newland. The building of the church was also made possible through the unqualified support and tangible assistance of miners who lived in the area. One miner even gave the field in which the church was erected.

Of the road which meet at **Christchurch** one leads to the Forest Enterprise camp sites and this is well marked. Another indicates 'Hillersland 3/4' 'Symonds Yat 2 1/2'. This road is the recognised and much used approach to **Symonds Yat Rock**. It does carry a weight restriction.

The Rock is possibly one of the best known and most visited beauty spots. It is also a place much favoured by rock climbers.

All the area, including the Rock itself, comes under the auspices of Forest Enterprise. It is well and thoughtfully maintained and managed. There is usually a member of the Forest Enterprise Staff on duty to give information and supply literature about the area. There are toilet facilities here and a small shop which sells some refreshments, cards, and souvenirs. There are excellent parking facilities for which there is a charge. A way marked trail starts from this point. During the season one of the greatest attractions for visitors to Symonds Yat Rock are the **Peregrine Falcons**. For some years the falcons have nested, and bred their young, high on the cliffs beside the river. They are amongst some of the Forest of Dean's most welcome residents. This sight of the young falcons making their first flight above the river valley is one which never fails to delight. The birds are protected and a constant watch is kept on them by members of the RSPB.

How Symonds Yat got its name is open to conjecture. The name Symonds is thought to have come from that of a previous owner. The word Yat means gate. Certainly it has been well known to previous inhabitants of the locality.

The Rock is the major viewpoint but there is another well worth making a short detour to enjoy. From just beside the small shop a track leads down to this vantage point. In wet weather this track can be a little slippery so caution is advised. Even so it should not be missed as it gives a view of the river from quite another angle. The approach to the Rock itself begins by crossing the main road by way of a log bridge.

A wall has been built around the perimeter of the Rock viewpoint for safety reasons. This is no way detracts from the wonderful view it commands of the River Wye and surrounding countryside.

Understandably, it is often thought that this stretch of the Wye between Ross and Monmouth is one of the most beautiful in the country. It is enchanting. The road down to the riverside from the Symond's Yat Rock is interesting. It is still the B4432. Because it is descending through rocky and steep terrain there is often only room for one vehicle but passing areas have been made at strategic points. The riverside area, immediately north of Symond's Yat Rock, which is encompassed here by the loop of the Wye is

The Huntsham Peninsula

Turning to the right, at the bottom of the road leading off the Rock just a little further along is **Huntsham Court**. This belongs to the Vaughan family of the Courtfield in Lydbrook. It has been in their possession since 1650. The entrance gates are unusual in that they are topped by the head of a deer made of metal.

The Wye Valley Farm Park, for rare and endangered breeds of farm animals, is located here. The Farm Park has been created by Richard and Sue Vaughan whose ancestors have owned the farm since 1650. Set in and around the magnificent old red sandstone farm buildings is a collection of rare and old fashioned farm animals. Children can get close to, touch and feed many of these beautiful farm animals including Suffolk Punch and Percheron heavy horses, Longhorn cows and calves, pigs and piglets, goats and numerous breeds of domestic poultry. Children can play on the new children's play area and picnics can be had in the farm yard or down by the river. There is a shop selling refreshments and souvenirs.

Huntsham Hill was a focal point for Neolithic and early Bronze Age peoples.

The **Queen Stone**, a large monolith away across the fields near the north end of the loop of the river, obviously had some significance in those ancient times. It could have marked a trading area or a place for ceremonial gatherings. It has also been thought to have been a place of sacrifice used by the Druids. The deep grooves which have been made in this ancient stone gave rise to such theories. Recent archaeological research would suggest that there is an ancient sacred site associated with every large loop of the Wye in this region. Near to Huntsham Court a Roman Villa was excavated in the 1960's

Return to the point where the road from the Symond's Yat Rock, instead of making the right turn to the Huntsham Peninsula, turns very sharply left. This leads only to: **Symond's Yat East**

This is a place beloved of visitors to the area. Here there is a camping site with facilities for caravan and tent. There is also a good number of hotels and places that cater for those who wish to stay a while. It is a lovely spot. People who wish to just sit and dream can

watch the river traffic. In the season pleasure boats carry people up and down the river. They go as far as the rapids. There are also canoeists who favour the Wye for their activities. It is possible, at this point, to cross to the other side of the river, Symond's Yat West, by hand-operated rope-ferry. The place is especially delightful in the warm months of the summer, when the hoteliers enhance their premises with hanging baskets and well filled gardens.

The railway tunnel, which once ran beneath the cliffs to emerge here, has been lost forever. A Hotel now stands where the mouth of the tunnel once was. The old track on which the trains ran is now a splendid path for walkers. Following this track, on foot, the **New Weir** rapids are just below Symond's Yat East. They are caused by the division of the river as it flows around a small island. These rapids provide a challenge for the canoeists. At this point the river flows through the heights of the Doward on the west and the cliffs of the **Seven Sisters** on the east.

About 1 1/5 miles on down the river is the **Biblins**. This, like all the woodlands hereabouts, belongs to the Forestry Commission and is administered by Forest Enterprise. Here it is possible to cross the river by rope suspension bridge. On the opposite side there is a log cabin provided for schools and group use for organised holidays. There are also facilities for camping. In this stretch of the Wye is **St. Martin's Pool**. It is said to be the deepest part of the River Wye.

Continuing along the old railway track the woods on the east are the **Highmeadow woods**. In the woods here, the area of forest known as **Lady Park Wood** has been left to nature. Since 1944 it has been a non-managed area of forest. It has been left by the Forestry Commission to develop naturally. English Nature do surveys of this area, which is in the region of forty acres, fairly regularly. It is a place not to be used by the general public without specific permission.

In about ³/₄ mile on the opposite side of the Wye, open fields may be seen in which once stood the **Hadnock Roman villa**, while towering above on the west bank is the **Little Doward** which contains, on its summit, the ramparts of an Iron Age hill-fort. Just before reaching the **Wye Bridge** at **Monmouth**, the small **Dixton Church** is passed. It is believed to be on the site of a monastery which was founded A.D. 735.

Most people travelling to Monmouth from the direction of English Bicknor, would continue on the B4228, through Christchurch, to where it joins the A4136. Here the road is signposted to Monmouth.

On this road the route is through farmland and then well forested land. Just after the lights at a road junction, on the right beside the road, the **Staunton Longstone** can be seen standing on the edge of woodland.

The Staunton Longstone is said by some to be the centre of the **Forest leylines**. It is also supposed that in ancient times it could have been a mustering point. A popular legend tells us that if pricked at midnight of the summer Solstice it will bleed and then take itself off down to the river to wash off the blood.

Staunton

Once known as Stane-ton - or a place of stone, Staunton is indeed a place of stones. High on the hilltop above Staunton meend is the **Buckstone**. Today the Buckstone lies just below the summit of the hilltop, firmly secured in its present position. The Buckstone was not

The Buckstone

always where we find it today. Once it stood upon the very summit, 891 feet above sea level, and it was a logan which is to say that it rocked on its base. The eminence on which the Buckstone stands commands some of the most extensive views to be found anywhere. The view extends to the **Malvern Hills**, the **Blorenge** near Abergavenny, **The Sugar Loaf**, the **Skirrid** and the **Black Mountains**. The very position of the Buckstone, perched so precariously atop one of the heights of the Forest land, was enough to give rise to a number of legends. It was said that anyone particularly evil would cause it to rock of its own volition if they went near the stone. There were other legends relating to the druids who were supposed to have worshipped there.

In the year 1885 there were actors, from a travelling company, staying in Monmouth. After the evening show they came up to the Buckstone and dislodged it from its precarious perch. The Stone split. It was restored by the Crown and secured in the position we find it in today. The Forest has lost, for ever, its rocking stone.

The meend, above which the Buckstone stands, now belongs to the people of Staunton. One of the few pieces of common land, of any size, in the Forest of Dean to be 'privatised'.

Just outside Staunton, at the bottom of the hill on which the Buckstone stands, is the Toad's Mouth Stone. It stands where the path for walkers leads up to the Buckstone. This stone can be seen from the Monmouth road. From a certain angle this rock jutting out of the hillside looks like the head of a giant toad. It is thought to have had some ritualistic importance in prehistoric times.

Down in the Highmeadow woods, immediately behind the village of Staunton, is the **Suckstone**. This is a huge piece of rock thought to have broken off the ledge behind. It is said to be the largest single block of stone in this country. Behind the Suckstone are the **Hearkening Rocks.** Here the keepers of the Forest used to wait and listen for poachers. The Hearkening Rocks act as a sounding board for any noises in the local woodlands.

The village of Staunton is old. It is on a cross-forest prehistoric route which was still used in the Roman period. Sections of old paved road can be found in the woods to the north of the present road between Staunton and Monmouth. Roman coins have also been found in the village of Staunton where, no doubt, the outcrops of iron which occur there were once worked.

The actual village of Staunton is on the opposite side of the road to the Church and is very pretty, nestling as it does beneath the hill on which the Buckstone stands. Staunton is very much a peripheral village of the Dean. The church of **All Saints** originated in Norman times. It dates from 1100 and is known as the 'Mother Church of the Forest'. It has a rarity; the medieval pulpit is made from stone. This is one of about sixty such pulpits in the country. There are two fonts in Staunton church. The one now being used is medieval.

In the churchyard is the grave of **David Mushet**. He was an ironmaster of some renown who came to live in the Forest of Dean in 1810. He made his home in Coleford. It was said that the arrival of David Mushet in the Forest heralded the beginning of the Industrial Revolution in that place.

David Mushet lived from 1772 -1847. For many years the Society of Metallurgists placed a wreath on his grave to mark the anniversary of his death.

On a green bank just outside the church gate is the remains of a 600 year old stone cross.

The A4136 road, from Staunton to Monmouth, is all downhill. There are some quite dangerous bends on this road. One of these bends is known, for obvious reasons, as 'The Fiddler's Elbow'. Just before Monmouth, on the last bend on the road, there is a sign which indicates a road to the **Kymin** (from Cae Maen-stone field). The rather hair raising ride up to the top of the Kymin, which is 820ft above sea level, is well worth while. From this point there are truly extensive

views to be had and many people visit just to enjoy the view. This area now belongs to the National Trust. The prominent buildings on the summit include a **Round House**, built in about 1793 by a wealthy Monmouth businessman as a summer house. In 1800 a Naval Temple was built here to commemorate the British Navy. Medallions name sixteen British admirals, including Nelson, who fought sea battles between 1759 and 1801. Nelson received the freedom of the Borough. He was said to have attended a public breakfast on the summit of the Kymin. He also made some rather derogatory remarks about the state of the Forest of Dean during his visit to Monmouth.

The town of Monmouth lies in the valley between the **River Wye** and the **River Monnow**.

The area West of Wye.

Wilton

Wilton stands just across the river from Ross. It was once quite an important place with its own castle. It is thought that the **castle** was built in the thirteenth century. Unlike all the other castles on the Wye, Wilton castle was built on low land beside the river not on some eminence. It was probably built at this point to guard a ford across the river. During the conflicts of the Civil War the castle was burnt by the Royalist Sheriff of Herefordshire, Sir Henry Lingen, in 1645. The last owner of what was left of the castle and the surrounding land was Thomas Guy. He left the land, and the ruins of the castle, to the London hospital which he founded and which bore his name. Today some of the ruins of the castle can be seen upstream of the bridge. The area is not open to the public. A private residence has been built on part of the site.

Wilton Bridge carries traffic to and from the Herefordshire side, into Ross on Wye. The bridge was built in 1599 after a terrible disaster happened. A ferry boat, the only means of getting across the water at that time, capsized with a considerable loss of life in the swollen waters of the river.

During the time of the plague in Ross, this bridge was the barrier between the country people and the pestilence which had afflicted the townspeople. The country people would bring their goods to the bridge at Wilton, and the townspeople would put money for the food received in bowls of water or vinegar, in the hope that this would disinfect the tainted money.

There is a **sundial** on the bridge. It was given by a certain Jonathan Barrow. It bears this inscription -

Esteem thy precious time,
Which pass so swift away.
Prepare then for eternity.
And do not make delay.

The Wilton side of the River Wye has much to offer. It is a most salubrious place to live. It is extremely pleasant to visit, with the proximity of the river and the good number of excellent eating places in the vicinity.

Bridstow is about three quarters a mile beyond Wilton in the direction of Hereford. Off the A48 it is tucked away in a hollo down a leafy lane and would be easy to miss. After crossing the bridge, go straight on to the roundabout, then turn right at the bottom of the village by the school. Close beside the Wells Brook is Bridstow church. It was an early Welsh church although none of the structure of the original church remains. It was dedicated to **St. Bridget** (Freit, Brigid or Bride) hence Bridstow, 'The sacred place of Bride'. The foundations of the present church were laid immediately prior to the Norman Conquest. There were many old and interesting features in the church. When it had an extensive renovation in 1860 many of these features were incorporated into the new structure. The churchyard cross shaft is probably fourteenth century but it now supports a sundial.

Bridstow is a small Herefordshire village in a delightful setting. The brook, which runs through the

Goodrich Castle

village, quietly makes its last journey through the fields to join the wider waters of the River Wye.

Bridstow is now the headquarters of 'Wye Valley Aviation' who are specialists in the field of aviation and especially in balloon flights. Flights take place in the morning from **Ross Sports Centre** near Wilton Bridge. In the evening the flights take off from the **Chase Hotel** in Ross on Wye. To continue the journey down the west of the Wye it is necessary to return to the roundabout at Wilton and take the A40 heading for Monmouth. The road passes through Pencraig. Just beyond is the turning to Goodrich.

Goodrich

The castle of Goodrich can easily be seen. It stands high above the River Wye in a commanding position. Even though it is now in ruins the castle is still most impressive. It is thought to have been built in the twelfth century and from its position it was, clearly built to guard a crossing of the Wye. It was one of the main residences of the famous William Marshall who was given the castle by King John. Marshall was one of the most influential men of his time. He was the only man at that time, other than royalty or clergy, to have a comtemporary biography written about him. An interesting local legend tells us that soil was brought from Ireland to make the floor of the castle so that no toads would live there. This may tie in with the fact that Marshall had extensive landholdings in Ireland.

During the Civil War it was garrisoned by the Parliamentarian Earl of Stamford. It very soon passed into the hands of the Royalists, and at the end of the war was under command of Sir Henry Lingen. With his troops he held out, with the castle besieged by the Parliamentarians under Colonel Birch. He finally had to surrender when the castle was bombarded with the 200lb mortar shells of 'Roaring Meg'. This gun was almost certainly cast in the Forest of Dean. It can be seen in the grounds of the **Churchill Gardens Museum** in Hereford.

Goodrich Castle is now looked after by English Heritage. It is an ideal setting for the pageants which take place there from time to time. The castle has been much renovated and is extremely interesting to visit. There is a well in the courtyard which drops to the level of the river.

It was in the courtyard of Goodrich Castle, which he was visiting on one of the celebrated Wye Tours, that the poet **William Wordsworth** met the little girl who inspired him to write the famous 'We are Seven' poem. It was published in 1800. The last lines of the poem read -

"How many are you then" said I,
"If they two are in heaven?"
Quick was the little Maid's reply,
"Oh Master we are seven."
"But they are dead. Those two
are dead.
Their spirits are in heaven"
'twas throwing words away; for still
The little maid would have her will
And said "Nay we are seven."

The village of Goodrich, with its delightful hostelry, is well in keeping with the ancient castle. The parish church of **St. Giles** at Goodrich is famous for the fact that, from 1628 to 1646, the Reverend Thomas Swift was vicar of the parish. He was the grand father of Dean Swift. Because his support for the Royalist cause in the Civil War he was turned out of the living. The chalice which was used by the Reverend Thomas Swift eventually came into possession of Dean Swift. He dedicated it to the service of Goodrich for ever. It is amongst the treasured possessions of that church.

Following the B4228 road towards the **Kerne Bridge** there is, on the left, the **Flanesford Priory**. It was founded in 1346 by the Augustinian order at a time when Goodrich Castle would have been an important fortress. There was a ferry crossing of the river at this point. What remained of the Priory, mainly the refectory, was used as a barn until in these more recent years it has been renovated and made suitable for living accommodation.

It was here at Goodrich that Henry of Bolingbrooke, Duke of Lancaster, used the ferry in 1387 to cross the river. He was told by the ferryman that his wife, in Monmouth, had given birth to a son. This so pleased the Duke that he granted the ferryman, and his family, the right to operate a ferry here for all time. The child was to become **Henry V of England.**

The area, which is here encompassed by a huge loop in the River Wye, is **Welsh Bicknor.** It has much of interest to offer. It can be approached by walkers along a pathway beside the river. It can be visited by car on a small road from the village of Goodrich. On the road through Goodrich there is a turning, not far from the school. This leads over the bridge which spans the B4228 road just outside Goodrich. It is not a through road. At points along this road it is possible to look down upon the river as it flows under the Kerne Bridge. The houses on the east bank can, from this place, be seen to better advantage and their superb position overlooking the river appreciated. This road over Coppit Hill leads through woodland and farmland to Courtfield. It was in this **Courtfield House** that Henry V was brought up as a child. Henry V was born in **Monmouth Castle.** At that time the area of Welsh Bicknor, which included the mansion house, belonged to Lady Margaret Montague who was

a descendant of Edward I. Henry V was nursed at the house in Welsh Bicknor by Joanna Waring.

In 1562 John Gillow of Hereford was Lord of the Manor of Welsh Bicknor. He had a daughter named Sybil. In 1563 she married James Vaughan, who came from ancient Welsh lineage. They came to live at Courtfield and from that time the Vaughans lived in the fine mansion house on the height of the point of Welsh Bicknor peninsula, commanding views over the Wye and pleasant land around.

In 1830 John Francis Vaughan of Courtfield married Elizabeth Rolls, daughter of John Rolls of the Hendre near Monmouth and aunt to Charles Rolls of Rolls Royce fame.

This marriage united two rich and powerful local families. Shortly after her marriage Elizabeth Rolls, known as Eliza, became a Catholic. For the rest of her life she was a devout and deeply committed member of that Church.

John and Eliza Vaughan had a large family. Eliza died giving birth to their fourteenth child. Of these fourteen children, six sons and four daughters were to spend their live in the service of The Roman Catholic Church. All were to distinguish themselves by the way in which they fulfilled their vocations. The eldest son Herbert

Vaughan was to become the most eminent of the family. He founded the **Mill Hill Missionary Society**. He had many important posts including that of Bishop of Salford and Archbishop of Westminster. In 1895 he became a Cardinal of Rome.

In 1895 Cardinal Herbert Vaughan laid the foundation stone for the new Westminster Cathedral which was built largely through his tireless efforts. He died in 1903.

Of the other sons, one was an archbishop, one was a bishop, the other three served the Catholic church as priests.

Of the daughters, one was a prioress, the other three served the church as nuns.

In 1950, Courtfield was sold to the Mill Hill Missionary Society. There is a small Roman Catholic church at Courtfield. From besides the main entrance gate to Courtfield the road winds steeply downhill to the small settlement of Welsh Bicknor. This is the goal of the walkers who followed the river path from Goodrich or beside the bridge at Walford. Welsh Bicknor can also be approached, on foot, from the east side of the River Wye. This crossing is a little up river near the factory where there is a disused railway **'Black Bridge'** over which it is possible to cross from east to west. There are camping facilities at Welsh Bicknor.

This quaint and enchanting place seems to have been caught in a time warp. It is so completely removed from the madding crowd and the hurly burly of this modern life it seems almost too good to be true. The downhill journey, from Courtfield, is a little hazardous but the place is well worth the effort made getting to it. There are houses built into the hillsides and they must all have an extremely pleasant view over the river to the hill beyond. At the bottom of the hill there is a Youth Hostel. The church stands at a distance from what was the big house and is now the Youth Hostel. It stands in the meadowland which borders the Wye at this place and is slightly raised. This may have been done with foresight because the river here does have a tendency to overflow its banks in times of flood. It is easily seen from the other side of the river. Dedicated to **St. Margaret**, it is a Victorian restoration. It is of much older origins than its Victorian restorations would lead one to suppose. It is indeed one of the oldest churches in the area and contains the recumbent stone effigy of a lady in fourteenth century dress. There is no indication of who this is but it is supposed it could be a memorial to Lady Margaret Montague who owned the Welsh Bicknor estates when Henry V was brought there to be nursed in 1387. Lady Margaret Montague died in 1395. A silver chalice belonging to the church bears the date 1176. In the churchyard there is a very ornate Plague cross.

Roman coins have been found on **Coppet Hill** as well as a bronze dodecahedron. This is a twelve faceted object with apertures. It is not known what purpose this object would have served.

For walkers there is a very steep climb up Coppet Hill to the promontory on which Courtfield House stands. Then through pasture land and woodland back to Goodrich.

For the car borne, the same route must be followed to rejoin the A40 in the direction of Monmouth.

The next place of interest is Whitchurch off the A40

In Roman times **Whitchurch** was a very important iron smelting settlement. It obtained the iron ore from outcrops on the Great Doward from nearby. There have also been prehistoric finds in the area.

The church, dedicated to **Saint Dubricius**, stands close to the river. There is some thirteenth and fourteenth century work to be seen in the fabric of the church. The font is Norman. The base of the cross in the churchyard is fifteenth century. Whitchurch is so close to **Symond's Yat West** that the two seem to be almost one. The **Jubilee Park** is evidence of the fact that this is a much

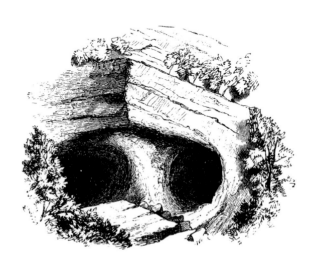

King Arthur's Cave

visited place. The Park has three major attractions which are appreciated by many people who come to this place. The **Wye Valley Heritage Centre** is a museum containing one of this country's largest collections of historic farm machinery and things from past ages. There is also the **Jubilee Puzzle Hedge Maze** and the **World of Butterflies** which is a huge glasshouse in which are kept an extraordinary collection of exotic tropical butterflies.

Symond's Yat West is just a continuation of Whitchurch except it nestles rather closer to the River Wye. It is here that the river begins its journey through the narrow gorge formed by thickly wooded cliff and high ground on either side. In the season there are pleasure **boat trips** up and down the river from this point. Reminiscent of many smugglers tales the **Old Ferrie Inn**, with fifteenth century origins, stands beside the river, a favourite spot in the summertime. Here the river can be crossed on request by a hand operated ferry. The Wye here proves that she is indeed 'The Queen of Rivers'. The scenery is quite breathtaking.

'King Arthur's Cave'

King Arthur had many caves between here and through North Wales. How this particular cave got its name is not known. It can be found situated above the **Severn Sister's Rocks** in a gently sloping bank in the wooded hillside. There is a small Forestry Commission car park, at map reference SO 5485 1585, by the side of the winding road which rises from Crocker's Ash and leads to the Biblins. By keeping the open fields to the right in view, it should not be too difficult to locate the cave which is only a very short distance from the car park down a well trodden path.

The cave in the limestone rock has been a shelter for man and beast for many thousands of years. This place has been a source of fascination for people for a long time. In 1870 it was seriously investigated and the floor of the cave was blown up by dynamite. There were found the bones of mammoth, woolly rhinoceros, deer, wild hyena and other species now extinct or no longer indigenous. There is a walk that can be taken from King Arthur's Cave along the top of the Seven Sisters Rocks which is quite breathtaking. It looks down on to the very deepest part of the Wye.

The summit of the **Doward Hill** is the site of an Iron Age hillfort. Legend says that this is where the famous Welsh Leader Caractus made his last stand against the Romans. As a result of that battle the field beside the river acquired its name of 'Slaughter'. The Doward is, perhaps, at its best in springtime when there is a wide variety of flora and grasses growing in the surrounding woodlands.

The **Biblins,** with its camping site and swing bridge, is reached by following the track down from the small car park. This is truly walking country when everything can be seen to its best advantage.

Returning to the A40 continue on the dual carriageway towards Monmouth for some short distance. Just past the road bridge there is a turning to **Ganarew.**

A few yards up this road to the right are the impressive gates and Lodge House of **Wynastone Leys.** The house is splendid. It stands in the wooded hillside high above the Wye which curls through the fields below. For some time Wynastone Leys was the home of A. Bonar Law who was Conservative Prime Minster of Britain from October 1922 to May 1923. Today, the 'Private Property' signs, are a forceful deterrent to the curious. Some of the grounds of the estate are now a nature reserve. Wynastone Leys now belongs to Nimbus Records of Monmouth. At this point the road branches to lead to Ganarew over the flyover across the A40. The church at Ganarew is on an ancient site.

The A40 continues in the direction of Monmouth and an imposing red dragon sign on the side of this dual carriageway informs that it is 'The County Of Gwent - The Gateway to Wales'.

Outside Monmouth the A40 diverts on to a roundabout. The first turning to the left is signposted 'Dixton'.

Dixton is a very small place at the end of a short length of road leading off the A40. It was obviously 'set aside' when the nearby road was improved. It is now a charming backwater which is unaffected by the rush of traffic on the A40. The little church is approached through a gated walk. It is a very ancient building. Most of the time **Dixton Church** would seem to be in a lovely spot beside the river. Sadly bacause of its position on low lying land, this little church has suffered a great deal from the floods which often fill these fields. Brass plates recording the height of the last three high water floods are on the north side of the chancel. The flood level of the 1960 high water is to be seen on the outside wall of the vestry.

In the porch is a list of the vicars who have served the church. They date from 1257 with William De Conflens, Archdeacon of Hereford, afterwards Bishop of Geneva.

It is overlooked from the hillsides by **Dingestow Court.**

MONMOUTH - CHEPSTOW

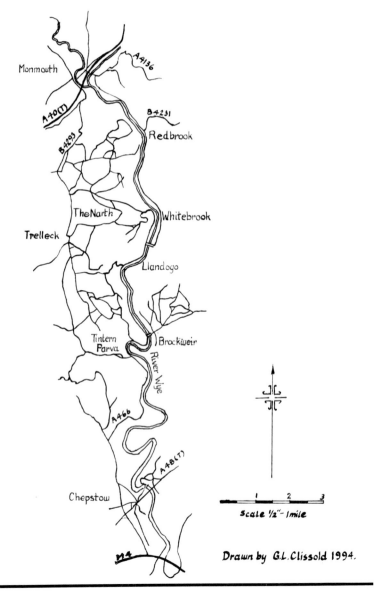

Monmouth

A4136

A40(T)

B4231

B4293

Redbrook

TheNarth

Whitebrook

Trelleck

Llandogo

Tintern
Parva

Brockweir

River Wye

A466

A48(T)

Chepstow

M4

Scale ½"- 1mile

Drawn by G.L.Clissold 1994.

Monmouth
to
Chepstow

MONMOUTH

Ross - 11
Hereford - 17
  (A466 light traffic only)
Abergavenny - 17
Chepstow - 16
Tourist Information -
  Shire Hall, Agincourt
  Square,
Cattle Market - Monday &
  Friday
Street Market - Friday &
  Saturday
Early Closing - Thursday

See Gazetteer for leisure and
recreational facilities

Any visitor to Monmouth would be left in little doubt that the place had strong connections with Henry V, for the very heart of this thriving border town is **Agincourt Square**. The square is looked down upon by a statue of Henry V, set into the front wall of the **Shire Hall**. The Square, previously Market Place, had its name changed at the time of the celebrated Wye Tours as a historical attraction for the tourists. At the same time the name of Inch Lane became Agincourt Street and another street had its name changed to **Glendower Street**. Much more impressive is the statue to the **Hon. C.S. Rolls**, which stands in front of the Shire Hall, appropriately holding an aeroplane. The Rolls family lived for some years at The Hendre, just outside Monmouth.

The Shire Hall, which is in the heart of Monmouth, was built in 1724 in place of a much smaller Elizabethan building. Once the Assize Courts were held here and in 1839 some Chartist leaders, including John Frost, were tried here for treason. Events leading up to the trial are brilliantly and movingly portrayed in Alexander Cordell's novel 'Rape of the Fair Country'.

Now, at the Shire Hall, is the Council Chamber, the Mayor's Parlour, the Office of the Town Clerk and the Tourist Information Office.

Much of the life of Monmouth revolves around this central area. Here the street markets are held and close by is a former eighteenth century coaching inn. Amongst the many famous people to stay in the Beaufort Arms was **William Wordsworth** the poet. He came to Monmouth twice in his twenties and again when he was in his seventy-first year. Sadly, this historic inn has been converted into flats and shops. They make a pleasant walk-through area. Tea, coffee and food can be obtained here and, in the warmer months, food can be taken sitting outside.

The Punch House Inn is another popular place in Monmouth. It stands alongside Agincourt Square. Here, weather permitting, drinks and food can be taken in the cobbled courtyard of the inn and

MONMOUTH

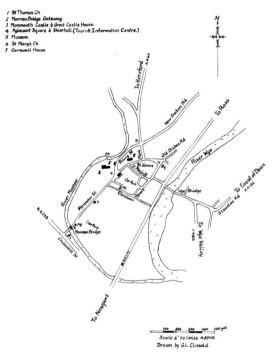

Street map of Monmouth

customers can watch the world go by in Agincourt Square. This inn was known as the Wine Vaults until its name was changed in 1896. On the opposite side of Agincourt Square, facing the Shire Hall, is the **King's Head Hotel**. This was also a coaching inn in the nineteenth century. From this inn a coach called **'Paul Pry'** left on a regular basis to travel to London. It went via

Ross, Gloucester, Cheltenham and Oxford and took eighteen hours to make the journey. It is claimed that **Charles I** visited the King's Head during the Civil War. Another distinguished guest was **William Cobbett**, a well known journalist and political writer who achieved fame for his 'Rural Rides'. He gave a lecture at the King's Head in 1830 and charged the audience an entrance fee of 2/- per head.

Another coaching inn was the **Queen's Head**. These inns were of great importance to the life of those who lived in that day and age and Monmouth, standing as it does strategically at the gateway to Wales, was a busy place. This is why it had so many coaching inns. Oliver Cromwell is said to have patronised the Queen's Head. **The Robin Hood** in lower Monnow Street is of great antiquity as can be seen from its sixteenth century arched doorway and internal moulded ceilings. It was here, from 1740, that the Catholics of the area met in an upstairs room hidden away at the end of a corridor to celebrate Mass. This was during the fifty years before the Catholic church was built.

Monmouth still has plenty of inns and hotels but not as many as there were in the eighteenth century. In the year 1722 there were 85 flourishing inns and beer houses in the town. In 1830 the number had dropped to a mere 47, but it is noted that the business of 'Landlord' was the main occupation recorded in the town. Competition was fierce and reputations jealously guarded. When the ostler at the White Swan drowned in a copper vat of beer, the landlord was quick to announce through the columns of the local paper that ... 'The whole of the beer in which the unfortunate victim drowned last week was all thrown away.'

Nelson came to Monmouth, probably one of the town's most eminent visitors. He came sailing up the Wye on the 25th July 1802. He was accompanied by his brother and sister and Lord and Lady Hamilton. They were greeted by a tremendous crowd. Both banks of the river, for two miles, were lined with excited people.

The Mayor and Common Council were waiting to welcome the distinguished visitors and the band played 'See the Conquering Hero Comes'. The party were taken, headed by the town band playing 'Rule Brittania', to the Beaufort Arms. They also visited the Kymin where Nelson said that it was not only one of the most beautiful places he had ever seen but, to the honour of Monmouth, the only monument to the Navy in the whole Kingdom

Dinner began at the Beaufort Arms at four o'clock in the

afternoon. All the local dignitaries and civic leaders were in attendance. Toasts and speeches were made and after the formalities were over Lady Hamilton, much to the delight of the assembled gathering, sang her own version of 'God Save The King'-

Join we great Nelson's Name
First on the roll of Fame
Him let us sing;
Spread we his praise around,
Honor of British ground,
Who made Nile's shores resound
God save the King.

Nelson was made a freeman of Monmouth.

From Monmouth, Nelson and his party left for Rudhall and Ross. Three years after coming to Monmouth, Nelson died. His memorable visit was never to be forgotten by the good people of Monmouth. His health was often drunk - at the Beaufort Arms - and on civic occasions. His visit was to inspire Lady Llangattock of Hendre, to collect memorabilia of the life of the great admiral. This included such things as letters, Nelson's sword, models of his ships, medals, posters and even Nelson's glass eye. So many things which had connections with his naval career and items which were of personal significance to the great man. The town was extremely fortunate in that, after the death of Lady Llangattock in 1923, her daughter gave to the town of Monmouth this absolutely unique collection. It is now in the **Nelson Museum** which is the only museum of its kind in the country.

The Nelson Collection and the Local History Centre is in **Priory Street** which leads off Agincourt Square. The museum is open daily including Saturdays. There is a charge for entrance, but children are admitted free if accompanied by an adult.

One of the most important families to live in the area of Monmouth were the Rolls family. They came to live at the **Hendre**, one of the finest estates in Monmouthshire, in the year 1830. The residence was converted by J.E. Rolls from a 'shooting box' to a splendid country house. It stood in a thousand acre deer park.

The Rolls family entertained the rich and famous including royalty. **King George V,** when he was Duke of York, came to stay at the Hendre. In 1892 J.A. Rolls was created a Baronet and he became Lord Llangattock. The family were great benefactors of Monmouth. The Rolls Hall, which is now the **Monmouth Library**, was given to the town by Lord Llangattock in 1887 to commemorate the Victoria Jubilee.

Perhaps the most famous of the eminent Rolls family was the Hon. Charles Stewart Rolls. He was a pioneer in the field of motoring and aviation. He died in an air crash at Bournemouth. The inscription reads -

Erected by public subscription to
the memory of the Hon. Charles
Stewart Rolls, third son of
Lord and Lady Llangattock,
as a tribute of admiration for his
great achievements in Motoring,
Ballooning and Aviation.
He was a pioneer in both scientific and
practical motoring and aviation, and
the first to fly across the
Channel from England to France and
back without landing.
He lost his life by the wrecking
of his aeroplane at Bournemouth
July 12th, 1910. His death caused
worldwide regret and deep
national sorrow.

Charles Rolls will always be remembered. He looks down upon Agincourt Square dressed in the clothes he wore on his cross Channel flight and many people who pass that way recall his commendable contributions to life as we know it today. The Hendre is now the **Rolls Golf Club.**

St. Mary's church in Monmouth is in an ideal situation. It is not too far from the centre, yet surrounded as it is by the large area of churchyard, much enhanced by the splendid copper beech and several flowering cherry trees, it seems to be an island of peace amid the busy everyday life of this border town.

The 200ft spire of the church is almost a landmark in this area lying between the two rivers. The first church was built on this site in about 1100. It was built to serve the **Monmouth Priory** alongside. The church was known for its **'Capper's Chapel',** for Monmouth was famous for the making of caps .. round knitted caps which were described as '.. the most ancient, general, warm and profitable covering of men's heads in this island'. In the sixteenth century it became the law of the land for everyone to wear a cap on highdays and Sundays with the exception of ladies and gentlemen of rank, who even so did wear the celebrated Monmouth Caps. It was noted that the 'Capper's Chapel' in the original church was richly decorated.

After the Dissolution when the Priory was suppressed, the church was much neglected. In 1736 it was rebuilt. Some of the Norman work was preserved. Then in 1882 the church was again rebuilt. Some of the beautiful medieval tiles from the previous buildings can be seen around the fourteenth century tower and some have been re-set in the south aisle. Set in the west wall is a Norman respond, a half pillar. There is also a stoop for holy water and a cresset from the original church building.

The remains of the **Old Priory** alongside the church, now a Youth Hostel, has given its name to the street on which is stands - Priory Street. There is an oriel window in the building claimed for many years to be the window of

Geoffrey of Monmouth's room and known as **'Geoffery's Window'**. He was the man who in 1136 wrote The History of the Kings of Britain. It has now been found that the window is of a much more recent date.

Henry V was born on 9th August 1387 at **Monmouth Castle**. The site of the castle was the high ridge above the **River Monnow**. The castle at Monmouth was built in 1071 and although it was an important border castle there is no doubt that its fame came mainly from the fact that this noble king was born within its walls. In the Civil War, Monmouth Castle changed hands several times and at the end of the war the walls were 'slighted' or damaged. The effects of negligence and damage inflicted at the time of the Civil War were serious. The castle was in a serious state of disrepair. The last private owner of the castle was the Duke of Beaufort who was an important landowner in the area. From the stones of the castle he built The Great Castle House as a town house.

Great Castle House is a truly splendid building. It has many commendable features including some beautiful, ornate ceilings. This lovely old house has had many uses over the years. Now it is the Headquarters of the **Monmouthshire Royal Engineers**, the senior Reserve regiment in the Army. In the building is the Castle and Regimental Museum. The few remaining ruined walls of the castle are enclosed within **The Great Castle House Garden**. The Museum is open to the public, who can also visit the gardens where only plants are grown which were known to have been growing at the time of Henry V.

The Great Castle House can be found from Agincourt Square. On the opposite side to the Shire Hall is a narrow road which leads up to the house and remains of the castle.

Monmouth is a town of surprises. Not only has it had a great deal to do with the making of history, but it is a place which still has some surprisingly fine houses and buildings.

The well preserved Great Castle House is an wonderful example of fine architecture. Many of Monmouth's other excellent buildings are well worth looking at closely. Despite the efforts of modern day architects, builders and, in most cases, a change of use, these superb building still stand as monuments to a much more gracious way of life and a much more imaginative and lasting way of building.

Travellers passing through Monmouth on the A40 cannot fail to notice, as they pause at the traffic lights outside the town, the building on the right. This is the **Monmouth Boys School**. Now a well known public school it is an old established school which was founded in 1615. It was William Jones, who came from Newland and built the almhouses there, who gave money for the building of the first Monmouth Boy's School. William Jones made his considerable wealth from trading. He belonged to the **Worshipful Company of Haberdashers**. He was a good christian man. William Jones also caused the almhouses in Monmouth to be built at the same time as the founding of the Boy's School. The almhouses are now an integral part of the Boy's School. In 1861 the Worshipful Company of Haberdashers rebuilt the School. Since that time it has continued to educate boys.

Agincourt Square, Monmouth

At the other end of town, on the right of the Hereford road, is the **Monmouth School for Girls**. This was founded, not without some local opposition, by the Worshipful Company of Haberdashers in 1892. The fine building we see today, high on the hill overlooking the town, was not finished until 1906. Both these buildings are well in keeping with the other fine buildings which grace Monmouth.

Monmouth Hospital stands near the site of the old gaol. Here the most famous prisoners were the Chartist leaders and others convicted in 1839. Although Frost, and two of the others held, were condemned to death, their sentences were commuted to transportation. They were shipped from nearby Chepstow to Van Dieman's Land, which is now known as Tasmania. Once Monmouth was served by the railways. The beautiful run up the Wye Valley from Ross through Symond's Yat came to May Hill, Staunton and Monmouth. It was first opened in 1876 and the last train left Chepstow, via Monmouth, for Ross on 15th January 1959. The closure of this line through such spectacularly scenic river valley must be one of the most regretted cuts of the 'Beeching Axe'.

Monnow Street is one of the best known streets in Monmouth. It makes a good entry to the town from the direction of Wales and stretches from Agincourt Square down to the **Monnow Bridge**.

Since the mid-1980s, when shop developers were attracted by the long burgage plots on Monnow Street, volunteer members of **Monmouth Archaelogical Society** have been kept busy with excavations which have revealed an enormous amount of previously unrecorded information about Roman and, especially, medieval Monmouth. Because of flooding the street was constantly being repaired. This meant that house and shop floors were being

raised with doing much of Monmouth's past was being buried.

From time to time the sites of these excellent excavations are open to the public and prove to be a source of great fascination.

Monmouth was known as the settlement of **Blestium** in Roman times.

On the left of Monnow Street just before the bridge is the **cattle market**. This was built to replace the market that, for many years, was held over the bridge in **Overmonnow**. There is a good parking area at the market.

The Monnow Bridge stands astride the river Monnow and funnels the traffic in single file through its arched opening. There is a walk through for pedestrians. Once Overmonnow was separate borough from Monmouth. Today it is an integral part of the town of Monmouth. Originally the Monnow Bridge gatehouse was a wooden structure. There were four gateways to Monmouth but there is only one left. The stone edifice we see today was built in the thirteen century. It is a wonderful bit of Monmouth's past history which has, fortunately, been preserved and saved to be appreciated by present and future generations.

The Bridge gatehouse has been much altered over the years and used for many purposes such as a private dwelling, a gaol, a guard house and as a militia store.

Overmonnow was once the centre for the making of the famous Monmouth caps.

This area has also been subjected to serious flooding problems getting the excess water from the Monnow and the Wye. The worst flooding to be suffered in Overmonnow, in the twentieth century, was after heavy snows of 1947. Almost half of the houses there were seriously affected.

The Overmonnow church of **St. Beckett,** was restored in 1874, the original building dating from 1186. It has a very curious font.

Monmouth is very fortunate in that **Keith Kissack**, a local historian, has written many informative books about its history. He has provided a wonderful record of how life evolved in this quite exceptional and fascinating border town.

Leaving Monmouth through the Monnow Bridge, turn left on to the B4293. This road crosses over the A40. From this point it is apparent that the A40 bypasses the town of Monmouth and entrances and exits from that place have to be carefully executed to find the right route.

Soon after the **Troddi Bridge** is passed on the B4293, the road branches off left towards Trellech. The bridge spans the **River Trothy**. This river joins the Wye just beyond the point where the waters of Monnow also enter those of Wye. The Trothy runs close to **Troy House**, another of Monmouth's fine buildings. This mansion house was built by the Duke of Beaufort in about 1673.

The road ascends for the next few miles and there are, from this vantage point, superb views back over Monmouth as it lies cradled between the hills of the Forest of Dean, the Kymin and the rising heights towards Hereford.

It is well worth visiting **Trellech** which lies on the plateau between Monmouth and Chepstow.

To get to Trellech continue on the B4293 until you come upon this now rather sleepy, ancient village which is steeped in history and legend. One unique claim to fame is that it was the birthplace of **Bertrand Russell**. This Welsh philosopher, mathematician and prolific author was an extremely controversial man. He was born in 1872. His parents died when he was still young and he was brought up by his grandmother. For some time Bertrand Russell was an active pacifist, but he renounced pacifism in 1939 with the rise of Fascism. In 1949 he gave the first BBC Reith Lecture. He was awarded the

Nobel Prize for literature in 1950. Much concerned with nuclear disarmament he played a leading role in CND. He succeeded his elder brother John as the 3rd. Earl Russell but continued to be known as plain Bertrand Russell. Late in his life he went to live in North Wales where he died in 1970 at the age of 98.

Trellech is situated on a one time Roman road which ran from Monmouth to Chepstow. It is set in lovely countryside and the first sight of Trellech is the church spire. An early christian church was known to have been established here in 755. The present day **church**, which is an ancient building, is surprisingly large. This reflects the fact that Trellech was once a much bigger and more important place than it is now. On farmland in the village can be seen a large earth mound known locally as **Terret Tump.** This is obviously a burial ground of some antiquity. It has been claimed that this is the place where the dead from the fighting forces of Harold Godwinson were buried, when the English were defeated after a bloody battle fought around Trellech. It can be reached via a footpath running alongside the parish church.

About 200 Yards along the road from Trellech, towards Llandogo, can be found the well of **St. Anne.** It is a chalybeatic spring impregnated with iron deposits from the bog ore which occurs here. It is known locally as the **'Virtuous' well.** Many years ago this well was a place of pilgrimage, for the waters were said to have healing properties. There were also legends which told of fairy visits on Midsummer nights to drink from its wondrous waters.

The most intriguing of Trellech's relics are the **Harold Stones.** These three stones stand, somewhat drunkenly, in a field alongside the B4293 as it leaves the crossroads in Trellech for Chepstow. They are known as Harold's stones since they are claimed to mark the scene of Harold's defeat in battle. This claim is quite wrong. The Harold Stones are of much older origin and date from Neolithic times. Legend tells us that these three stones are here as a result of Jack o'Kent's continuing feud with the devil which seemed to be a long run contest to see which of the two could throw large stones the furthest distance The redoubtable Jack was claimed to have thrown these three stones from **Skirrid**.

In the churchyard there is an early preaching cross. Within the church there is a most unusual sundial which is octagonal in shape. On three sides are noted the mysteries of Trellech: **The Tumulus** on the farmland, the **Standing Stones** and the chaly beate spring. On the fourth side is acknowledged the fact that this interesting sundial was given to the village in the seventeenth century by Lady Magdalen Probert. The upper part of the sundial, where each face is inscribed with the hours, bears the thought provoking words -

The hour in passing consumes
the passing day.

Retrace steps back along the B4293 towards Monmouth. About a mile and a half from Monmouth on the left is the sixteenth century **White House Farm**. From here there are splendid views across the Wye Valley and over the Forest of Dean. The panoramic views also extend into Wales where, on clear days, the **Brecon Beacons** and **Black Mountains** can be seen. To the left there is a minor road which is signposted Penallt. In 1982 a remarkable finely flaked Neolithic flint arrowhead, 57mm long, was found near here. This is evidence of a very early use of this area. On this road, at the **Croes Vane** crossroads, is the old **Bush Inn**.

Penallt is a village standing high above the Wye on the opposite side of the river to **Redbrook**. The **Argoed**, a particularly fine house, is one of Penallt's most famous buildings. It dates from about 1580 when it was built by Christopher Probert. It fell into a state of disrepair and was restored about 1860 when Richard Potter, chairman of the Great Western Railway, lived there with his family

of nine daughters. Many famous and distinguished people visited this place to enjoy its beautiful situation and the fine grounds. Amongst those who came to stay at Argoed were founder members of the early Fabian Socialists. They included **George Bernard Shaw** who wrote *Arms and the Man* here. Bernard Shaw was awarded the Nobel Prize for literature in 1925.

Penallt has another curious connection with the past. It was a place where mill-stones were made. These stones were made in the village, atop the high riverbank, and then rolled down to the river to be sold. Today many of these large stones can still be seen in the river.

At the crossroads keep straight on and down Lone Lane. This is a very narrow and steep lane overhung in the summer with an excess of vegetation, but with a few passing places. It descends for about 650 feet to the banks of the Wye opposite Lower Redbrook which is England.

Here can be found **The Boat**, an inn tucked away under the hillside beside the Wye. Parking outside of this intriguing public house is very restricted and its proper car park is some distance away. Even though The Boat is in Wales, its car park is in England, beside the A466 Monmouth to Chepstow road. From the car park The Boat has to be reached by crossing over a footway of the disused railway bridge over the River Wye. It must be one of the most unusual approaches to any public house.

Before the advent of the railways The Boat was dependant upon the river traffic, although there was a ferry across from Redbrook.

Redbrook was once a heavily industrialised area. It wanders down beside a road which leads from Newland in the Forest of Dean. Along this road can be seen the leats and water reservoirs which were used in the industries which flourished here. There were iron forges, and copper tinplate was also produced here. **The tinplate works** closed in 1961 was the last tinplate works which used the hand process to close in this country.

From The Boat continue back along the lane which begins to ascend towards the church. There are some isolated cottages and along the roadside are some very large stones. These are known locally as packing or pecking stones.

It is just over one mile to '**The Old Church'** of Penallt. It stands in splendid isolation on a promontory overlooking the Wye. The lych gate leads to the entrance. On the door of the church is carved the date 1539. The tower, a chancel arch and parts of the north wall date from the late thirteenth century. The muniment (document) chest is carved from a solid oak trunk and possibly dates from the twelfth century. There are many other things of great interest in this old church, although much was lost during the restoration of 1887. In the churchyard are the remains of what was probably a fifteenth century cross.

There is an old stone mounting block in its original place.

Continue up the hill over **Church Hill Common.** At **Penygarn** head for the B4293, towards Trellech. An ancient inn **The Gockett** is passed on the right, near which is the point where five parishes meet. This is marked by an inscribed stone on the left of the road.

In just under a mile turn left towards the **Narth** and **Whitebrook.** Continue straight on at the first crossroads down the Whitebrook valley. This is an enchanting place, a wooded gorge through which runs the 'White Brook'. The wooded hillsides are dotted with charming cottages, ruined walls and beautifully landscaped, stone lined pools. These are all the remains of furnaces, mills and millponds.

In the seventeenth century German expertise was brought here to establish a wiremaking industry which would utilise the water of the White Brook to provide water powered forges. It became the **Tintern Wireworks Company**. These wireworks closed about 1720 and in 1760 paper making was to take its place. Six or seven paper works were set up, again utilising the waters of the White Brook. The remains of these industries have in no way detracted from the beauty of the place. At the bottom of this lovely valley the road merges with the A466 Monmouth to Chepstow road.

To return to Monmouth on the east of the Wye it is necessary to turn left and pass over the **Bigsweir Bridge**. Because of the restricted width of this bridge there are traffic lights to control crossing. Just at the traffic lights there is an empty toll house, whose long gone occupant once operated the toll system. The road to the right leads through a high banked heavily wooded area and opens out into the village of Llandogo.

The houses of **Llandogo** climb up the heights of the hillside to look down upon the A466 and the River Wye. It is a place which has attracted and held the love of many people. Llandogo is the final point of the tidal backwash from the Severn which washes up the Wye from **Beachley**. It makes the place more easily navigable but also leaves behind the legacy of tidal flow - some mud.

The tide brings, in the spring, **elvers**, those multitudes of slithery string-like young eels which miraculously make their way from the Sargasso Sea. The Wye also has that king of fish, the salmon, as an indigenous frequenter of its waters.

Visitors are well catered for in Llandogo. There are several hotels and a motel. This is a wonderful area for walking. **The Wye Valley Walk** follows a woodland route here high above the River Wye. Tumbling down from the heights above Llandogo are the **Creddon Falls**. They are a series of cascades that descend over 500 ft in half a mile. From here the walker may either explore to the north **Cuckoo Wood** or south through **Bargain Wood** following nature trails.

There is still in Llandogo some evidence of the use that was made of these upper reaches of tidal navigation. Once many small river craft visited this place. The quays which were beside the river have all gone, as have the beer houses which once served those who came here from the trows, barges and sloops which, obviously, gave the name to 'The Sloop Inn'.

Llandogo has a lovely **church**. It is often claimed to be the most interesting in the Wye Valley. The church lies to the left between the main A466 road and the river.

Old Brockweir

The church actually gives its name to the area because Llan is the old Welsh word for an enclosure or church, and Dogo was the name of the founder of the church. He was also known as Doden, or in Latin Oudeceus. He was the Bishop of Llandaff.

The church is well worth visiting because it has some particularly fine stained glass windows.

Built in the 16th century the original **St Oudoceus** church was replaced by the present building in 1860. The curvilinear churchyard still exists as testimony to the antiquity of the original church. There is also a very fine large yew tree in the churchyard. Between the church and the road is a pleasant area of green on which is the rather unusual War Memorial.

Just beside the church there is a 'walker's sign' which says that it is 1.4 km to Bigsweir Bridge.

A road immediately opposite the entrance road to the church leads off the A466 to Trellech and the Cleddon Falls. This is, of course, for anyone wishing to visit by car. The winding road up over the heights gives an opportunity to admire the beauty of Llandogo and the river Wye from several vantage points.

The people of the locality are well aware of the precious heritage of beauty and history which is theirs to preserve and hopefully pass on to future generations. For over twenty years there has been a Lower Wye Valley Preservation Society in existence. The aims of this society, which meets regularly, are to preserve the peace and tranquillity of the area and protect its natural beauty.

Continue on the A466 from Llandogo to the renovated bridge which crosses the river and leads to the very pleasant riverside village of **Brockweir**. Until the bridge was built in 1904, the river was crossed at this point by a ferry.

When river traffic was an important feature of commerce, Brockweir was a place where ships were built and restored. The place had a measure of importance in that there was a quay, and facilities for coping with the traffic of the river. Part of the quay can still be seen near the river.

Once Brockweir had an abundance of beer and cider houses. Today it has just one, the **Brockweir Inn**.

Still flourishing in Brockweir is a **Moravian church**, tucked away over a bridge which spans the lively brook which tumbles down the hillside to join the waters of the Wye. Behind the Inn and other riverside buildings the church stands in a very pleasant spot. It has the feeling of being well used and much loved. In the church burial ground is the grave of **Flora Klickman**. Her writing of such works as Flower Patch and Trail of the Ragged Robin and others of similar theme were inspired by her home surroundings in this lovely village of Brockweir. Other writers, including Rafael Sabatini, have found inspiration here, beside the quiet waters of the River Wye.

This is an ideal spot from which to explore the river side and surrounding countryside. The **Offa's Dyke Path** and **St. Briavels Common** route both meet here at Brockweir.

The A466 continues from Brockweir in the direction of **Tintern**. Just before reaching that place, to the left, there is signposted the **'Old Station Tintern'**. Until 1959 the **Wye Valley Railway** line, which closed in 1964, brought visitors to Tintern. The railway was first laid and operated by the Wye Valley Railway Company. When it was in financial difficulties it was taken over, in 1905, by the Great Western Railway Company. Today the old station, complete with railway carriages, serves as an information centre. Refreshments are available. There is also a railway exhibition and many things to interest all ages. The immediate vicinity of the Old Station is a very pleasant and well laid out picnic and barbecue area. The Old Station is the starting point for several walks through places of interest in the locality.

At the approach to Tintern can be found, on the left lying away from the main road, the ancient church dedicated to **St. Michael and All Angels.** On the spot where the church now stands, in the year 555, a hermit lived. By 765 a Celtic Church had been built there and a church has been standing there since that time.

Tintern Abbey

Through the centuries many changes have been made to this old church. The most radical of these changes took place in 1846, when a considerable amount of re-building was done.

There is no doubt that Tintern was known to the Romans. They introduced the **vine** in the Wye Valley. Today the vine is growing again in this area, for Tintern has, growing on a south facing hillside, a small vineyard. It is said that this is the site of a vineyard which once belonged to the monks of the nearby abbey.

From the grapes produced, on the sunny slopes which overlook the village of **Tintern Parva**, is made Tintern Parva wine. Behind the vineyard, on the heights above this area of the Wye Valley, are woods. The name of Barbadoes has been given to a particular hill and to a green in this area. It is a strange name to find in this quiet, typically English place. Possibly it has connections with some entrepreneurial man of the sea, or of business, who made money in that distant place.

The village of Tintern, now well interspersed with antique shops, tea rooms and such, leads the traveller to the ultimate goal of **Tintern Abbey**. From wherever it is seen this old building is awe inspiring. The roofless ruin of this twelfth century abbey has such an ambience of tranquillity and timelessness that even the clamour of thousands of visitors who come each year to see and pay homage cannot affect it. No matter how many day trippers and tourists come to gaze, the abbey stands aloof, alone, wrapped in its own particular aura.

These ruins have inspired many words to be written in its praise. Countless paintings have been executed in an effort to transfer to canvas the glory that is Tintern Abbey. Turner painted it in 1795. Visitors to the abbey are not only a feature of this day and age. The eighteenth century Wye Tours called at Tintern Abbey. The celebrated visitors who came this way would find that the ivy covered ruins provided shelter for an army of beggars. Hovels were built around the walls of the Abbey and many of the vagrants would offer their services as guides to the tourists. Today the immaculately preserved ruins are maintained and administered by Cadw Welsh Historic Monuments.

Close to the abbey is the **Abbey Mill**, probably not the original mill site of the monks but it overlooks the river and has several things of great interest. Bicycles can be hired here. There is on site parking. It is open every day throughout the year.

Tintern Abbey was founded in 1131. It was built under the supervision of monks of the

Cistercian order, on land given to them by Walter fitz Richard de Clare, Lord of Striguil, or Chepstow. The Cistercian Monks sought solitude and they found it here where the River Wye gently embraces the sweep of the land on which they raised their abbey. The tree clad heights on either side provided a measure of insularity. It was, at the time the abbey was built, a very isolated spot. Tintern was only the second Cistercian abbey to be built in Wales.

In the year 1270 Roger Bigod, who was then Earl of Norfolk, initiated a major re-building project at the abbey. This gave us the abbey, the remains of which we see today. The abbey at Tintern was wealthy in lands. At one time it owned considerable estates on both sides of the River, and over to the Severn, where lands around Woolaston belonged to the abbey. Further properties in Yorkshire and Kent were also acquired.

The fortunes of the abbey changed in the reign of Henry VIII. When his survey was taken Tintern did not have sufficient revenue to be allowed to continue as an abbey and so, in 1535, Tintern Abbey was dissolved.

Shortly after the monks left, the roof was lifted and through the years many of the stones were taken from the abbey to be used in buildings around the place.

It was the monks from Tintern Abbey who started industries in that area. Those industries continued after the dissolution of the abbey and brought considerable prosperity to Tintern.

Whitebrook and Tintern had wireworks, and the river at this point had a deal of traffic. At one time Tintern had an active wharf and docks which were much used.

A small plaque on the wall which surrounds the Abbey states that
> Near this plaque in the year 1568 brass was first made by alloying copper with zinc.

Tintern is well served with hotels, guest houses, and bed and breakfast accommodation. Opposite the entrance to Tintern Abbey is the **Beaufort Hotel**. Its name recalls the fact that until 1901, when the Crown were to acquire the estates, the Beauforts had been major landowners in this locality.

After the dissolution of the abbey the site and lands became the possession of Henry Earl of Worcester, and then passed to his descendants, the Dukes of Beaufort.

Leaving Tintern and travelling towards Chepstow the road winds upwards between woodland. On the right, woodlands cloak steep cliffs and, on the left beyond a belt of trees, there is a drop to the river in the deep valley below.

This is a spectacular drive at any time but in autumn it is at its best when thousands of trees flaunt the colours of the fall.

It was on wooded heights 'A few miles above Tintern Abbey' that **William Wordsworth** wrote his immortal poem when he re-visited the area during a tour in 1798.

> Five years have past, five
> summers, with the length
> Of five long winters, and again
> I hear
> These waters rolling from their
> mountain springs
> With soft inland murmur -
> Once again Do I behold these
> steep and lofty cliffs,
> That on a wild secluded scene impress
> Thoughts of more deep seclusion;
> and connect
> The landscape with the quiet of
> the sky.

On this road there are places for picnics and viewing. It is well worth taking some time to pause at one of the stopping places for there is, in season, a profusion of wild flowers growing in these woodlands. Nightingales also sing in these woodlands.

All the area around Tintern is wonderful country for walking. Indeed walking is the best way of exploring the ways and byways which lead through the woodlands

and quiet meadowland of this wonderful countryside. From near the abbey it is possible to walk to the **Devil's Pulpit** high in the wooded banks on the opposite side of the river. This is a venture not to be undertaken by those who have aversion to steep uphill walking! Waymarked paths enable those so inclined to walk along the top of cliffs from Tintern to the top of the Wyndcliffe.

For those who wish to travel by car there is a much easier way of ascending the **Wyndcliffe** or Wyncliff (there are variations on the spelling of this placename). **The Wyndcliffe Viewpoint** is the highest point of the cliffs which bound the A466 on the right coming from Tintern. At the top of this road, just past the first bend of the descent there is, on the right, a sharp turning with a sign that indicates Wyndcliffe.

A visit to the Wyndcliffe is a must for all who seek to see the beauty of the Wye Valley. The road, leading sharply from the A466, travels a short distance to a small car park. Here visitors are warned to 'Watch out there's a thief about'. From this car park in the trees high above the roadway it is a steady climb to the **'Eagle's Nest'** some 800ft above the river which winds its way through the valley far below.

From the Eagle's Nest viewpoint can be seen, weather permitting, the whole of the surrounding countryside. This superb panoramic view encompasses nine counties, the **River Wye, Chepstow**, the distant **Black Mountains, Malvern Hills** and the distinctive **Sugar Loaf**. From this vantage point can be seen, for the first time on this journey, the wide waters of the River Severn spanned by the silver link of the **Severn Bridge**. Completed in 1966 this bridge which carries the M4 motorway from England to Wales is an elegant feat of modern day engineering.

Leaving the Wyndcliffe to rejoin the A466 on the left almost opposite the Wyndcliffe turning is the pathway leading to the **Giant's Cave**. It is just a short distance from here to the pretty village of St. Arvans. The name of a public house **Piercefield Hotel** in the village of **St. Arvans** serves to remind those who pass by that the racecourse, on the opposite side of the road, was once the **Piercefield Estate**.

This lovely area along the banks of the Wye was, in the mid years of the eighteenth century, the home and estate of **Valentine Morris**. He had strong ties with the West Indies. He lavished a deal of money on his home and estates at Piercefield. To further enhance the beauty of the already lovely estate, Valentine Morris had the grounds laid out in the style of Capability Brown. The viewpoints in the park, which look over the surrounding countryside and river, were all laid out with a deal of originality, and were imaginatively arranged and called such things as the Grotto and other fanciful names. He also made the **Giant's Cave**.

For some years, in the 1870s, Valentine Morris was Governor of St. Vincent. Sadly he died in poverty.

Through the kindness and courtesy of the present owners of the **Chepstow Racecourse**, it is still possible to walk in this beautiful area. Here the river, bounded on the west side by the Piercefield Cliffs, with the **Twelve Apostles**, makes a wide sweep to surround the **Lancaut Peninsula**.

Left of the roundabout at the end of the road leading beside the Racecourse can be seen the impressive Lion's Lodge gates. From here it is a short distance to the old and fascinating town of Chepstow.

The Wye Valley

CHEPSTOW - FOREST of DEAN.

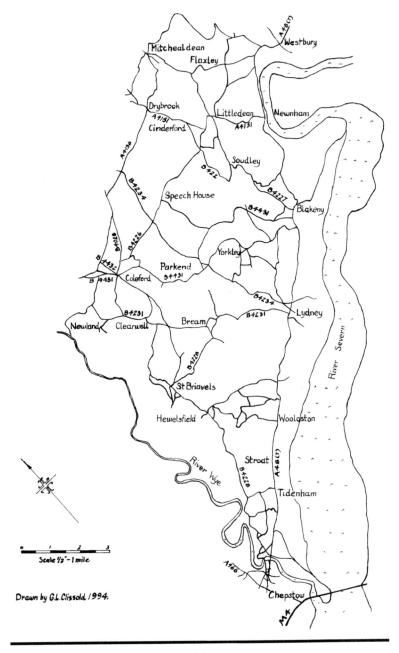

Scale ⅓" - 1 mile

Drawn by G.L.Clissold 1994.

CHEPSTOW
to
ST BRIAVELS

CHEPSTOW
Newport - 16
Tintern - 7
Monmouth - 16
Tourist Information - Castle Car Park - Bridge Street.
Market Day - Sunday at the Racecourse.
Early Closing - Wednesday - some shops.
Coach Park & Rest Room - Castle CarPark - Bridge Street.
Railway - Station Street.

See Gazetteer for leisure and recreational facilities

Chepstow is the gateway to Wales. It is an impressive entrance to that country and should ideally be approached over the **Old Wye Bridge**. There are traffic lights at the approach to the bridge which sometimes give a brief time to observe the castle. At this point there is the best possible view of the ruins of **Chepstow's Castle**, set on a spectacular position on top of the cliffs which rise from the river. If, however, the town is entered from the direction of Tintern it is usual to come on the A48 which now intersects the town.

The area of Chepstow has been a settlement for thousands of years. In the locality has been found evidence of Iron Age and Roman occupation. The name of **Bulwark**, given to a residential area of the town, takes its name from a near by Iron Age encampment: a circular camp surrounded by a ditch.

The Romans built a bridge across the river about half a mile upstream from the present bridge.

Even though the area was known to earlier settlers there is no doubt that Chepstow owes its presents origins to the Normans.

After the Norman invasion **William Fitzosbern** built, in 1067, a castle on the cliffs of the river at Chepstow from which to subdue the Welsh. It was the first stone castle built in Wales. In the twelfth and thirteenth centuries it was much enlarged.

In the thirteenth century a bridge was built across the **River Wye**. Having a limited life it was necessary to replace the bridge several times over the years. In 1814 a cast iron bridge was built in place of the previous wooden one, and it was opened officially. In more recent years a new bridge carrying the A48 into Wales has been built across the river and takes much of the traffic from the Old Wye Bridge.

Half a mile upstream from the present bridge the Romans had a bridge across the Wye.

The Old Wye Bridge is still in use. The centre of the bridge marks the official boundary between England and Wales. It is possible to stand in the middle of the bridge with one foot in each country.

The best place from which to start an exploration on foot of

CHEPSTOW

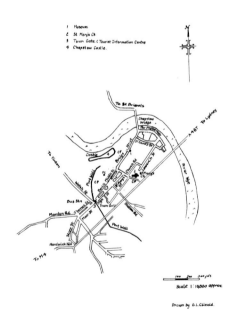

Street map of Chepstow

Chepstow is the castle car park. There are three **Walking Trails** which take those who follow them through some of the most interesting parts of Chepstow.

This car park area is well placed and well suited to deal with the many visitors who come to Chepstow. The excellent **Tourist Office** (which opens seasonally) is sited here. Just across the street is the **Chepstow Museum**. Since 1983 the museum has been based in the **Gwy House**. Built in 1795, until it became the Museum Gwy House had strong associations with the medical profession and was for some years the **Chepstow Hospital**. Visits to the castle also start from the car park.

Chepstow Castle dominates the town. Even in partial ruin it still has a situation and presence which conveys the fact that it was once a place of great importance. It has always been a stronghold and a place which intimidated those who would have attacked it because of its position and strength.

At the time of the Civil War, Chepstow and the castle were owned by the Marquis of Worcester who supported the Royalist cause. It was the scene of several bloody battles for the castle was in a strategic position. It was held to siege twice and eventually fell to the forces of the Parliamentarians. After the Civil War, the castle reverted to the Marquis of Worcester. In 1682 Henry, Marquis of Worcester, was created Duke of Beaufort. The family held the castle until 1914.

In the late years of the thirteenth century Chepstow was needing protection from the landward side. A defensive wall was built known as the Portwall and much of it still stands. It can be seen around a part of the castle car park.

The entrance into the town through the Portwall was by way of the **Town Gate**. The original gate was built at the same time as the wall but it was rebuilt in the early sixteenth century. This lovely medieval Town Gate has had many uses other than for which it was made. For some time it was a gaol. Now, standing between **Moor Street** and the **High Street,** the Town Gate straddles the road and restricts the busy traffic to single flow.

Because of its position on the tidal and navigable River Wye, Chepstow has had long and strong links with shipping. It even had, at one time, its own **Custom House**. What remains of these times now past can be found around 'The Back' which simply means a wharf. Once this now quiet place bustled with activity generated from the business of loading and off loading cargo from the ships which operated in and out of Chepstow.

The early name for Chepstow was Striguil. The Saxons called it Chepe-Stowe a market place or place of trade. Once there was a dry-dock at the riverside where ships were repaired, but there is no trace of this once all important area. It is almost impossible, looking at The Back today, to realise just how things once were, with the river crowded with shipping and works on the banks beside the river.

There is just the **Boat Inn** to serveas a reminder that once this was a place of boats.

Shipbuilding was revived briefly in Chepstow during the First World War. It was necessary to build houses to accommodate those who came to work in the shipyard. A residential area was built at the Bulwark.

The parish church and priory church of **St. Mary** stands where the first house of religion wa s founded, by William Fitzosbern, at the same time he built the castle. Built by **Benedictine Monks** it was for some time a priory of that order. The priory was suppressed at the time of the dissolution of the monasteries by **Henry VIII**. Major restoration work was done on the church in the nineteenth century.

One of the most interesting memorials within the church is that of **Henry Marten**. He was one of the signatories on the death warrant of Charles I. After the Civil War he was brought to trial and condemned to death. The sentence was never carried out. Henry Marten was imprisoned in Chepstow Castle where, with his wife, he lived in some comfort, in a part of the castle to become known as the Marten Tower.

Henry Marten lived as a prisoner for the last twenty years of his natural life. He died at the age of seventy-eight. His epitaph in Chepstow church where he was buried, is unusual in that the first word of every line spells his name.

Chepstow is a town which has preserved its past well whilst taking the present day, with its related problems, easily in its stride.

The town is built on a hillside. It seems that every street, by some means or other, finds its way downhill. One has even taken the highly descriptive name of **Steep Street**.

The eighteenth century local poet the Reverend Edward Davies wrote of Chepstow -

> He, who by land would enter
> Chepstow town,
> Must quit his horse and lead him
> gently down:
> The long descent so rugged is so
> steep.
> That even post-boys, here for safety
> creep...
> Cats with sharp claws, and nanny-
> goats in dread
> Descend the shelving street, and
> cautious tread.
> In this snug town good meat and
> drink abound,
> But, strange to say there cannot
> yet be found
> One single inch of horizontal ground.

There are some very elegant houses in Chepstow and also some very interesting houses. The Beaufort Hotel, situated in the **Beaufort Square**, was originally a coach inn. This square, in which the Beaufort Hotel now stands, was simply called The Square before Chepstow was re-organised to cope with present day life. It was then the heart and centre of the town of Chepstow. There are in this locality several fine buildings of the eighteenth and nineteenth century. The name of the hotel recalls that, for many years, the Beaufort family, as well as owning the castle, were also owners of a great deal of land and property in the Wye Valley.

Adjoining the Portwall is another hotel of interest, **The George**. A house of great character, built in 1610, The George was an inn and **Post House**, the first inside the Town gate.

Amongst the buildings of note are the **Montague Almhouses**. Built to be of benefit to the residents of Chepstow town, provision was made for these almhouses under the terms of the will of Sir Walter Montague. Of necessity these almhouses have been repaired and renovated over the years but still maintain much of their original facade.

At the top of **Bridge Street** can been seen the **Powis Almhouses** built in 1720. The money for the building of these Almhouses was provided by local man, Thomas Powis who left Chepstow and made much wealth in the wider world as a vintner.

One of the most charming areas of Chepstow must be **St. Mary's Arcade** and **St. Mary Street**. These places are now pedestrianised which helps those who visit to take a more relaxed and leisurely look at the individuality of the shops and houses.

There is an excellent town map at the top of St. Mary Street. It was painted by local artist Keith Underwood.

Chepstow is twinned with Cormeilles in Normandy. It was from the Abbey at Cormeilles that the Benedictine monks came, in 1067, to build the **Priory** on the site of the present Chepstow church.

In his lifetime **Ivor Waters** wrote a number of books covering many aspects of the life and times of Chepstow. He was a man who knew and loved Chepstow and he has left, for posterity, a wonderful record of his town.

Leaving Chepstow, **The Bridge Inn** down by the river, the first pub in Wales, is the last to be seen in that country before returning to England over the Old Bridge.

On the England side of the Old Wye Bridge the road rises in a long curve towards the village of **Tutshill.** At the crossroads in Tutshill it is advisable to take time to visit **Sedbury** and **Beachley.** The directions to these two places are clearly marked on the signpost at the crossroads. At a peninsula formed by the impending convergence of the Severn and Wye this area has an interesting history, for it has always been a place of strategic importance.

The **Beachley Peninsula** has, because of modern day changes, become rather a mundane area through which to travel. Just at the point where Sedbury links with Beachley, there is a drive leading away from the left to **Sedbury Park.** This prestigious house has played an important part in the history of the place for it had always been a residence of some significance even before it was bought, in 1825, by George Ormerod. On acquiring the house George Ormerod immediately changed its name to Sedbury Park. He then began to remodel the building on classical lines. In 1875 the house and estates were sold to Samuel Marling who was to become a baronet. Sedbury Park remained in the possession of the Marling family until 1921. Since that time it has been a hotel and an approved school for boys. Now it is a home for the elderly.

At Beachley the last section of Offa's Dyke, **Buttington Tump,** was intersected when the road to the point of the peninsula was widened in 1960. Offa's Dyke, which can be traced for 142 miles, ends here on the banks of the River Wye.

There was a Roman settlement on the Beachley peninsula. Traces of Roman occupation have been found around the area of Sedbury Park. The Romans also had a crossing of the river here from **Aust** to Beachley. It was from the Roman name given to this crossing that Aust has taken its name. It has always been claimed that it was near Beachley, in the year 603, that **St. Augustine** met the Welsh bishops in an attempt to settle their ecclesiastical differences. History records that the meeting was not a success.

Much of the area at the end of the peninsula is now the property of the MOD. Between 1927 and 1994 this was the home of the **Army Apprentice College.** Approaching the farthest point of the peninsula one is more and more conscious of the Severn Bridge. The whole place is dominated by the spectacle of this tremendous engineering feat.

The road ends at a small car park immediately under the bridge. Beside the car park are the remains of the slipway which once aided the loading of the ferries which plied between Beachley and Aust taking cars and passengers across this treacherous and very unpredictable stretch of water.

The ferries were first started in an organised and commercial manner in 1827 and were sponsored by the then Lord of Tidenham Manor, the **Duke of Beaufort**, who was also the major landowner in the whole area.

The crossing was a very hazardous one. It could take as long as five hours to cross depending on the vagaries of the tides and wind. There have been many accidents on this stretch of river and two major tragedies. Although there is no access to the bridge from Beachley it is very much a part of the life of the place.

The **Severn Bridge**, linking England with Wales, is suspended some 400 feet above the turbulent waters of the Severn which, because of the intrusion of the Beachley Peninsula, is narrowed to about a mile. The towers of the bridge are 455 feet high. From beneath the bridge can be heard the ceaseless rumble of the traffic which has been travelling across the bridge ever since it was opened on 8th September 1966 by Queen Elizabeth II.

Almost beneath the bridge are the headquarters of SARA, the **Severn Auxiliary Rescue Association.**

From the car park beneath the bridge there is a walk beside the Severn leading past the small power station on the river bank. On this point can be seen the ruins of **St. Tecla's Chapel.** It is thought to have been the site of a beacon set there for the benefit of mariners in this dangerous stretch of water. From this place can also be seen the meeting of the Severn and Wye. These two rivers rise together in the heights of **Plynlimmon.** At Beachley they join to form the **Bristol Channel.** Returning to Tutshill, at the crossroads, follow the road straight across and head for Woodcroft.

The settlement of **Woodcroft** straddles the road for some way. What is not immediately obvious is the fact that the River Wye is very close. On the left of the road at a small brown sign indicating 'Sedbury Cliffs 2 ' there is an almost hidden gap at the side of the road. This could accommodate three parked cars but is a rather precarious parking place because of its proximity to the main road. This is the approach to **'Winter's Leap'.** There are several paths along the top of these tall cliffs which are immediately behind the roadside houses. The view from this place is truly spectacular. It overlooks a wide bend of the river. On the other side is a point of the **Chepstow Racecourse** estate (once the Piercefield estates). When the tide is full this area is filled with water. When the tide is out the mudbanks are exposed and the wildlife, particularly birds, are to be seen in abundance.

This stretch of the river cliffs takes its name from **Sir John Wintour** or Winter. He was, at the time of the Civil War, a leading Royalist with a mansion home at Lydney. It must be remembered that prior to the Civil War John Winter had owned the Forest of Dean and had been responsible for decimating that place. It was said that his axe-men had felled all but two hundred of the Dean's fine trees and, in consequence, Sir John Winter was not in favour with the people of that place. Added to that the Forest of Dean had been mostly in sympathy with the cause of the Parliamentarians. **Whitecross**, the home of Sir John Winter in Lydney, was attacked by the Roundheads. He was forced to flee. He rode on horseback from Beachley and, hard pressed, found himself with his enemies in hot pursuit behind and the steep cliffs of Woodcroft in front. Still on horseback he went over the cliffs. By some miracle he slithered and slid down the cliffs to safety at the river. Here he was taken on board one of the Royalist ships which were lying at anchor in the river.

Today at Winter's Leap there are no knightly escapades - just the clink of crampons and shouted instructions for these steep cliffs are now the haunt of the experienced rock climber.

Until 1959 the railway track from the Monmouth to Chepstow ran beside the river beneath these cliffs. Continuing on this road, shortly after leaving Winter's Leap there is a road to the left signposted **Lancaut**. This leads to a sparsely populated area beyond which is a greensward. On this cars may be parked whilst the more energetic make their way to the river some distance below. The road leads on past the green area. It is a narrow road which passes through some lovely woodland. It must be noted that this whole area is a **Gloucestershire Wildlife Trust Nature Reserve**. There is a small settlement and a farm at the end of the road. From here a path leads down over a field to the river. This point gives a superb view of the **Woodcroft cliffs** and **Winter's Leap**.

Almost hidden amongst the trees at the edge of the river are the fast decaying ruins of the church of **St. James**. The remains of this church stand as a monument, a sad reminder of the life that once existed and thrived here. The settlement that was once here was of Celtic origin. There is a walk near here said to be the path taken by the Monks from **Tintern** when they visited Lancaut.

Amongst the interesting items still to be seen in the ruined church is a bowl which once contained wine, or vinegar, into which the lepers, for there was said to have been a lepers colony here, dropped their offerings to be disinfected. The furnishings and other artefacts have long since been removed from this small church. The lead font is in Gloucester cathedral. The gravestones, which were removed from the churchyard, have been returned and now stand within the disintegrating walls of the ivy covered ruin.

Across the river are the fields of what was once the Piercefield estates. The main road from Lancaut leads towards **Tidenham Chase**, a place which was previously the hunting ground of the Lords of Striguil, as Chepstow was once called. Tidenham Chase is still a wooded area, now under control of the Forestry Commission.

Between the main roadway, the B4228 and the River Wye, there are identifiable stretches of **Offa's Dyke**. About 780, King Offa of Mercia built his dyke which stretches from the River Dee to near the mouth of the River Wye. It was thought to have been made either as a defence or boundary between Wales and Mercia.

In places at Tidenham Chase the earthworks of the Dyke reach as much as twenty feet high with a trench of some considerable depth as well. It could be that Tidenham Chase was one of the first places

to be inhabited by man in the area. It was a wild and lonely place. Excavations of a tumulus on Tidenham Chase has provided evidence of Mesolithic and early Bronze Age settlers. There are also signs of an early trackway leading from the banks of the Severn over the Chase to Brockweir on the Wye. At Brockweir there was a crossing place. Where there are gaps in the woodlands at Tidenham Chase it is possible to get lovely views over the **Severn Vale**, for Tidenham is part of a large peninsula formed by Wye and Severn. Tidenham Chase also has its own church. This is fairly modern, dating from the late nineteenth century. This church lies beside the B4228 and is beautifully maintained. It is dedicated to **St. Michael** and was built by Gambier Parry.

The village of Tidenham has a much older church. This was mentioned in the **Domesday Book**. Even so, the present church dedicated to St. Mary dates from the thirteenth century. In the middle of the nineteenth century this church underwent extensive renovations.

The road continues through Tidenham Chase. There is on the left a good car and bus park set in Forestry land. It is from this place that it is possible to walk through the woods to the viewpoint, overlooking the River Wye, known as the **Devil's**

Pulpit. This place commands wonderful views over the river, and Tintern in particular. Legend tells that when the monks were building the abbey at Tintern the Devil stood on this eminence and tried to dissuade them from building this House of God.

There is also, on Tidenham Chase, a rather more modern standing stone. It stands in **Poor's Allotment** on the Chase. It bears an inscription VRI 1837-97. It was put there to commemorate Queen Victoria's Jubilee by a wealthy local family. Even though there are quite a few houses now built in the area known as Tidenham Chase it does still have an air of isolation which is a faint echo of how things used to be.

The B4228 road leads on from Tidenham Chase through farmland following the high crest of land between the Severn and Wye. Some miles along this road a crossroads indicates directions to Brockweir and Hewelsfield.

The small village of **Hewelsfield** is scattered but delightful. It is extremely rural, hiding amongst high hedges and quiet country lanes, and it has an ambience of great peace and tranquillity. The church of **St. Mary Magdalene** is the jewel in this very charming place. It is of very ancient origin. Saxon, possibly with even earlier beginnings, and certainly bearing traces of Norman influence. It

seems to crouch upon the green of the surrounding graveyard with the roof sweeping down to just a few feet from the ground. There is no doubt that Hewelsfield church is very ancient and that the rare circumlinear churchyard encompasses one of the oldest buildings in the Forest of Dean. Within the churchyard is a thirteen hundred year old yew tree, one of the oldest in the country. In the short tower there are six bells. One of these dates from the year 1450 and is the oldest ringable church bell in the Dean.

Leaving the joy of Hewelsfield and returning to the B4228 continue on this road in the direction of St. Briavels.

Although not strictly within the Forest proper, **St. Briavels** is the place which gave its name to the old Hundred which encompasses the Forest of Dean.

Standing some six hundred feet above sea level overlooking the Wye Valley, St. Briavels is in a place of some prominence. It can also be approached by the steep winding road which leads up from the bridge at Bigsweir which crosses the river Wye.

Built on a high plateau, the church and the castle at St. Briavels command views over the deep valley below. As well as being so integrated into the history of the Dean and having the only **castle** now standing in the Forest of Dean, St. Briavels is also a very pleasant place to live. In the years since the war it has grown with much new development.

Both the castle and the church have Norman origin although the church is much older than the castle. It is thought that it was possibly founded on a Celtic site.

There is no doubt that the incomparable position of St. Briavels, standing as it does overlooking Wales, was one of the reasons why, Earl of Hereford, chose to build his castle here in 1131. From this high place the defenders of the castle were able to see and be seen. It was said that this castle was built to deter the incursions of the Welsh. Certainly it was used to enforce law and order in the Forest of Dean. There are still obvious traces of the moat which once surrounded the castle. Much has been added to the original castle building. Most of what we see today dates from the thirteenth century. In the year 1276 the towers on either side of the present gateway were added. Since that time there have been many alterations and additions and, for many years, there was a great deal of neglect.

For a certain time each day, visitors are allowed into the courtyard of the castle.

In the wall can be seen the fireplace which is all that is left of what once was the great hall. King John was a frequent visitor to St. Briavels. Improved accommodation was built for him early in the thirteenth century. These Royal apartments, and what was once the chapel and the gatehouse, are still in use. Now they are utilised for a very different purpose because, in 1948, St. Briavels Castle became the first such building in the country to be converted to a Youth Hostel.

For many years St. Briavels Castle was the administrative and judicial centre of the Forest of Dean. On the south chimney can be seen a stone hunting horn. This was the symbol indicating that the castle was the official residence of the **Constables and Wardens** of the Forest of Dean. They were responsible for the overall management of the Forest. Even so, it was usually the deputies who carried out most of the often onerous tasks connected with this office. It was also the seat of judgement and a place of incarceration for those who offended. Penalties for the Foresters who dared to steal the King's deer (and they often did) were severe. The preservation of the chase was one of the Constable's duties. Those caught breaking the law had little compassion shown to them. It was said that outside the old courtroom was a pole on which nine offenders could be hung at once.

The castle was used not only by King John, but by many other royal and noble men, who came for the pleasure of hunting in the Forest of Dean. To the castle were also brought the grievances of the miners to be considered by the **Mine Law Courts** which were occasionally held here.

In the early part of the nineteenth century, the castle, by this time much neglected, was being used as a gaol for debtors. At a review carried out in 1832 it was considered to be too insanitary for such purposes so this use of the castle came to an end.

The parish church of **St. Mary the Virgin,** which stands exactly opposite the castle, still bears traces of Norman influence. including a Norman font. The church has a most unusual stone faced clock in the tower.

St. Briavels Castle

St. Briavels is a place of history and legend. It is claimed, by some

ancient right, that the people of the place have the exclusive right to take firewood from the **Hudnalls** which is a tract of woodland sweeping down from St. Briavels towards the River Wye. There were several stories and legends of how this privilege became the prerogative of the people of St. Briavels. Whatever the truth of it is, this privilege is treated very seriously by the people and they make every effort to guard their rights. They have a 'Keeper of Hudnalls', a king who has a crown albeit made of cardboard. His brief is to protect the special rights and see that no 'foreigners' take wood from the Hudnalls.

One of the most popular legends about the origin of the rights tells that the wife of Sir Milo Fitz Walter, Earl of Hereford, obtained this right for the people of St. Briavels by riding in the manner of Lady Godiva around the village. Her reciprocal conditions were that, in future, the rich of the place should feed the poor. There is to this day a tradition which is carried out on Whit Sunday after evening service in the church, when bread and cheese bought from money collected from the residents of St. Briavels is distributed.

Until the middle of the nineteenth century this distribution was done in the church where bread and cheese, after being blessed, was thrown to the people present. The ensuing scramble got so out of hand that a stop was put to this practice and the distribution was taken away from the church. Today, after evensong and the customary blessing, the bread and cheese is thrown by appointed distributors from a high wall outside the church.

Legend also says that King John, on one of his visits to the castle, heard about Milo's lady and her selfless act. He suggested that whenever he came to the castle perhaps the village maidens could be asked to emulate the noble gesture. There is no record that they ever did.

St. Briavels was also, after the thirteenth century, famous for making quarrels, or arrow heads, for the cross-bow.

The George Hotel, which stands not far from the castle, also has a very interesting history. It is probably comprised of several cottages claimed, by local legend, to have been ostler's cottages at the time when the castle was built and first used. It has definite medieval traces and there is, in the wall, a coffin lid of very ancient origin

The village today has a thriving community spirit. The present day inhabitants of St. Briavels are very proud of the important part their village has played in making the fascinating history of the Forest of Dean.

From St. Briavels there are two routes of interest through the Forest of Dean.

Route one is through **Bream,** to **the heart of the Forest.**

Route two is through **Coleford,** joining the A4136, to **Mitcheldean.** Down the **Flaxley valley** to **Westbury on Severn.** Take the A48 to **Stroat.**

Route one through Bream to the heart of the Forest.

At the crossroads in St. Briavels follow the road signposted **Bream.** This is an unclassified road through agricultural land. There are some very interesting farmhouses on this route. About $3/4$ of a mile from Bream, on the left hand side of the road, is the **Closeturf Farm.** This is an area which has been the source of much archaeological interest. At a short distance from the Closeturf Farm, and straddling the B4228 St. Briavels to Coleford road, is **Bearse Common.** This place has also been very rich in archaeological finds. It seems to have been a major Neolithic centre and trading post. In this area was found one of the finest examples of a polished flint axe of Neolothic age to have been found anywhere in the district. On the Bearse the **Longstone** once stood. Standing some nine to ten feet high it was of gritstone and was an excellent example of a standing stone. Sadly it was destroyed about 1875 by the then tenant farmer who considered it was a nuisance.

A short distance from the Closeturf Farm there is a T junction. Roads lead to **Aylburton** and **Bream**.

This is exceptionally pleasant countryside. The area is known as **Priors Mense**. In the valley there is an old and very interesting large house. It stands in extensive grounds and was, for many years, known as Bream Lodge. Today it is known as **Priors Lodge**.

This considerable, and very substantial house, dates back at least to the 16th century. In the late years of that century it was the residence of **William Pawlett**. He was Sergeant of Law and Deputy Constable of St. Briavel's Castle. William Pawlett died, at his house, in 1703. He was buried in Lydney. Today Priors Lodge is the home of one of the four Verderers of the Forest of Dean.

The road which leads from this place to Bream is narrow and for much of the way is between high hedges. Bream is entered opposite the Church of **St. James the Apostle**, on the B4231. Restoration and extensive building began on this church in 1822. This was instigated by the Reverend Henry Poole, Vicar of Parkend.

Previously the Bream Chapel, built in 1218, stood on this site. The rebuilt church was consecrated and re-opened on 13th October 1826.

Even though the present church is not old there are interesting silver communion vessels which are a part of the church's furnishings. They include a chalice inscribed with the words 'The gift of James Gough of Pastor's Hill, Gent and Mary his wife. To the Chapell of Breem 1680'. Also there is a silver paten or chalice

Bream Scowles

cover. This is inscribed with the initials of James Gough and engraved. Before the Civil War, the Goughs were people of some importance and status in the area of Bream.

Just a short distance out of Bream on the B4231 road to Lydney are the **Bream Scowles**. They are in the woodlands to the right of the main road. A cottage stands near the entrance. Access to this wooded area is by courtesy of the **Lydney Park Estates**. These woodlands are one of the few tracts of Forest land in the Dean which do not come under the auspices of the Forestry Commission.

Scowle is a word which is peculiar to the Forest of Dean. It simply means an open working. The scowles can easily be found in the Forest where they were worked. Look for huge holes gouged out of the surrounding woodlands. Many were used in Roman times and, occasionally, Roman coins have been found among the debris. Nature has now almost reclaimed her own. Trees and bushes grow from the strangely shaped workings in weird and grotesque ways making the place strange and rather mysterious. The early method of getting the iron ore from the earth of these scowles was crude. Fires were lit against the walls, the limestone crumbled from the heat, and the iron ore was exposed. It is said that when the early missionaries came to this place they passed through these dark woods where they saw little red men climbing out of the great smoke belching holes in the ground. They were the miners covered in the red ochre of the iron ore. The missionaries called them, for obvious reasons, The Red Devils.

Return to Bream on the B4231, turn right into the village at the T junction. On the right is the old **'New Inn'**. This is one of the most interesting houses in the village. The New Inn once belonged to the Gough family and was possibly built by them. It dates back to before the Civil War. On either side of the mantelpiece there is a device, or monogram, which bears the initials G.C. The date 1637 can also be seen. In more recent years the building belonged to the **Dean Heritage Museum** but it has now passed back into private hands.

Another house in the village, which could possibly be even older than the New Inn, is the public house once known as the Rising Sun and now called **The Village Inn**.

The **Pastor's Hill Farm** and the Farm at **Bream Cross** are all buildings of similar age. Bream is one of the largest of the forest villages. It lies upon a steep hillside. From the area of the War Memorial there are extensive views over the surrounding forest land.

The Forest of Dean actually covers about 27,000 acres of growing woodland with some waste or common land. The Dean is one of this country's smallest forests, but what it lacks in size it makes up for in age. The Forest of Dean is one of the few primeval forests still in existence in this country today. It is undulating country and from the vantage point of Bream can be seen, on the opposite hillside, the villages of Pillowell and Yorkley.

Leave Bream on the unclassified road heading towards **Parkend**. Here is a Forestry Commission sign which indicates that this is the threshold of the Forest.

The road to Parkend is through groves of oak trees. Sheep frequent this road because it is Forest proper. Commoners' rights apply and the sheep are allowed to wander at will. When the rights came into being they were said to apply to cattle, horses, donkeys (of which there were plenty in the forest), goats, pigs, fowl, ducks and geese. Sheep were said to be uncommonable animals. Today, there are about many thousands of sheep and very few other 'commonable animals' wandering within the boundaries of the Forest. These commoners' rights are not unique to the Forest of Dean.

At the junction with the road from Coleford, which is signposted to Parkend and Whitecroft, on the left there is one of the **old toll houses**, now renovated. These houses were used for the collection of tolls at strategic points on the Forest roadways until 1888.

On the left of the road leading into **Parkend** is the **Cannop Valley Nature Reserve** which includes the **Nagshead Nature Reserve**. This is managed in conjunction with the RSPB and is open to the public. The forest is rich in birdlife. As well as the peregrine falcons which now nest in the cliffs near Symonds Yat rock, flycatchers, firecrests, greater spotted woodpeckers, woodwarblers as well as indigenous jays, magpies and other birds can be seen in the woods around the Dean. Even kingfishers are occasional visitors to one of the ponds in the Forest. Buzzards have also been seen.

There is a sign opposite the bird reserve marked **CSMA**. This directs to a private leisure park owned by the Civil Service Motoring Association. The **Darkhill Brook** separates the Park from the main road. The area of the park is now 33 acres and it has excellent facilities for members of the Civil Service who camp or stay in chalets. This was once the site of the **Whitemead Park Lodge**. A fine house stood on this site. Built in the Middle Ages, Whitemead Park Lodge was used as a hunting lodge. The grounds were once very extensive. In the later years of its existence,

Whitemead Park Lodge belonged to the Crown and then the Forestry Commission. For some years it was the residence of the Deputy Surveyor of the Forest of Dean. The last Deputy Surveyor to live there was Mr. Sanzen Baker. In 1970 the house was completely destroyed by fire.

Parkend is a quiet, pleasant village. It has a Post Office, a craft shop and two popular public houses. Overlooking the old railway station site is an impressive house. Now a pleasant country house hotel, **Parkend House** was once the home of the prominent and successful mineowners in the locality of Parkend, who owned the **New Fancy pit**.

Those interested in industrial history should take time to pause in Parkend. It is the village nearest to the very centre of the Forest of Dean and stands amidst woodlands. The Parkend

area was known to the Romans. Last century a cache of many hundred of Roman coins were found at a site in the heart of the village where the present Post Office now stands. Now it is a peaceful place where a game of cricket is enjoyed. In the nineteenth century Parkend was a very different place. It was then one of the industrial centres of the Forest. There were quite important coal mines in the locality, and in the centre of the village was an **iron-works**.

In the year 1827 it was hoped to obtain the power to work the furnaces at the iron-works from a giant water-wheel. This was to be one of the largest in the country and was specially made in Gloucester. Permission was obtained to dam the brook higher up the **Cannop Valley** to provide the necessary volume of water to work the wheel. The giant water wheel was not a success. However the venture did give the Forest

the **Cannop Ponds** which were the result of the damming operation. Many generations have benefitted from the peace and tranquillity of these waters. All that is now left of the great industry which once thrived in Parkend is one of the engine houses. It is a distinctive landmark. A tall ivy covered building, it was renovated in the early years of this century. The chimney stack came down in 1908 when the re-furbishment of the engine house was under way. This building was to become the very first Forester Training School in the country now the **Dean Field Study Centre**.

The revival of the Forest of Dean Steam Centre began in Parkend before moving to Norchard near Lydney. In its industrial past, Parkend was well served with tramways and railways.

The woodlands through which the nearby B4234 passes are all a part of the Cannop Valley Nature Reserve which stretches from the Mirey Stock crossroads on the A4136 to Parkend. Some short distance beyond Remploy factory, on a slow wide bend, can be found the only stone cutting works now in operation in the Forest of Dean. It stands at the bottom end of the Cannop ponds which were formed to supply water to iron-works in Parkend.

On the opposite side of the road to the stone-works is a wide track into the forest. This leads up an area known as the **Bixslade**. Some of the stone used at the **Forest Stone Works** comes from the deep quarries at the top of this place. The start of this track is easily identified as that of an old tramway, perhaps the last to be used in the Forest. This is how the stone was originally brought down from the quarries to the Stone works. A few hundred yards up this track is the **Mine Train Quarry**. It is a working quarry which produces ornamental stone much used in gardens. Strangely, no planning permission was needed to work this quarry because it is within the Forest on Forestry Commission land so the free quarrying rights apply.

On the other side of this track can be found a **working free-mine**. It is one of the very few free-mines still working full-time in the Dean. This mine is very much a one man industry. Free mining rights are a privilege unique to the men of the Forest of Dean. The men of the Forest had always assumed a right to mine. This they had done from 'tyme out of mynde'. It is thought that, in the reign of Edward I, the men of the Forest of Dean had these ratified in royal appreciation of their bravery in battle. The regulations pertaining to these rights were set in '**The Book of Dennis'** which was virtually the miner's bible. The free-mining rights were revised in the 1832/38 survey. Today, to qualify for the right to free mine in the Forest of Dean a man has to have been born within the Forest which is measured by the old Hundred of St. Briavels. He must have worked, for one year and one day, in an iron or coal mine, or for free quarrying rights, in a stone quarry. He also must be over the age of twenty-one. This man can then apply in his own right to the Deputy Gaveller for a mine which he may work. The important change that came in relation to free-mining rights in the survey of 1832 was that whereas previously only a free miner should work a free-mine, the revision allowed that once having acquired his mine a free-miner could then sell that right. This has made it possible for such things as opencast to take place in the Forest. All that is needed is for the free-miner to take out a gale. Then if he so chooses he may sell it to some outside entrepreneur.

Return to Parkend on the B4234 and visit the Church of **St. Paul**. This is to the east of the village tucked beneath the skirt of the forest. This church, dedicated in May 1822, was built largely through the efforts of the Reverend H. Poole who was the first incumbent. He spent his life, and all his money, promoting the word of God in this place.

Continuing on B4234, the next village is **Whitecroft**. This village was once the home of the **Whitecroft pin factory**. It was also close to the site of one of the Dean's most prosperous collieries, the **Princess Royal**. This colliery closed in 1962.

Whitecroft, Pillowell and **Yorkley** all gently merge into one large ribbon of development which cuts through the woodlands from Whitecroft in the valley to the top of Yorkley. Yorkley perhaps took its name from the **York Walk** in which it stands. This is one of the six divisions into which the Forest of Dean was divided after the Civil War. At that time, after the decimation of the Forest under the ownership of Sir John Wintour from Lydney, it was felt that the Forest needed tidying up, so in 1668 an Act was passed allowing for the enclosure of up to 11,000 acres at any one time. This was to allow for re-afforestation. The plantations were enclosed to allow new growth undisturbed and the Forest was split into six walks. In each of these walks was built a substantial house. They were some of the first buildings of any significance to be built within the Forest.

The houses, or the lodges as they were called, were named after important people of the day. There was **Herbert Lodge** and the walk named after Lord Herbert. Latimer Lodge and the walk named after Viscount Latimer. **Worcester Lodge** and walk named after Henry Marquis of Worcester who was then Constable of the castle at St. Briavels. Danby Lodge and the walk named after the Earl of Danby who was, at that time, Prime Minister. **York Lodge** and the walk was named after the Duke of York.

Early in 1688 the people of the Forest were not feeling too happy about the King, James II. There was an uprising. Apparently as a protest against the King, the Foresters badly damaged the Speech House set in the King's Walk. They pulled down the Worcester Lodge as well as York Lodge which had been named to honour James II when he was Duke of York.

The differences of so long ago have all now been forgotten, Yorkley, Pillowell and Whitecroft have changed almost beyond recognition. All traces of the mining industry have virtually gone. Yorkley is still proud of the fact that it gave its name to one of the coal seams of the Dean. Pillowell and Yorkley will be well remembered as the last home of the Poet **F.W. Harvey**.

Will Harvey was not a Forester by birth. He was born at Hartpury and brought up in Minsterworth, fought in the 1914/18 war and found a measure of self expression during his time as a prisoner of war through writing poetry. Will Harvey was a gifted poet who loved Gloucestershire. When he was articled as a solicitor, he eventually made his home at Pillowell and Yorkley. Not only a poet but also a great music lover, Harvey had many contemporaries who shared his interests: Herbert Howells, Leonard Clark, Ivor Gurney, the Frith brothers and many others.

Each day Will Harvey went to follow his calling at his Lydney office. He found his recreation by joining in the simple pursuits of those amongst whom he lived. He joined the **Whitecroft Male Voice Choir**. Not only did he sing with them, but at local concerts he also entertained with his poems and often acted as compere. Even though he was not born a Forester, Will Harvey became very much a part of the Forest scene. He never forgot those he served with in the war and was extremely proud of his old battalion the 5th Gloucesters.

The Forest lost a friend and the world lost a poet, lover of music and a man who cared deeply about others when, on 13th February 1957 Will Harvey died at the age of 69.

Although Harvey will always be remembered for his famous poem 'Ducks' he did write of his home woods as follows-

'In Pillowell Woods'
(Dedicated to Franz Schubert)

To me they seemed like bluebells;
millions
Nay, myriads of bluebells... their
small chiming
Out-rang the peal of all the bells
of bronze
In all the world. But whether
'twas a chiming
For lover's living, or for lovers dead
Who knows in Pillowell where
the bluebells pillow well
A lover's drowsy head?

At Yorkley follow Parkend road to the next T junction signposted **Moseley Green** and **Speech House**. On this road is the small hamlet of Moseley Green. It is like a lost bit of the old Forest. A few cottages are clustered near the much renovated **Rising Sun** public house. Some years ago Moseley Green was featured in one of the quality Sunday newspapers as a bit of unspoilt England.

Continue on this road to the next T junction. Near here on the corner is a house which has been converted from what once was a Primitive **Methodist Church** built in 1908 to serve the local community.

To the right along this road in the woods can be found the **Mallard's Pike Lake**, which is signposted on the road to the left.

In the Forest of Dean there are no natural lakes or large ponds. All are man-made, mostly to serve some past industry. Mallard's Pike was not made for this purpose. It was actually made in the early years of the 1980s purely for the pleasure of the general public. It is a wonderful asset to the Forest of Dean and attracts a large number of visitors all year round. Ample car parking space is provided.

Following the main road the B4431 leads through pleasant forest land which still bears recognisable traces of past industry. On this road is the **Wenchford Picnic Site**. At the top end of this very well laid out site is a road which leads on a scenic drive through to Soudley. It is signposted **'Blackpool Bridge road'** and is entered by passing under one of the lovely old stone bridges which once carried the railway which ran through this part of the Forest. Beyond this bridge can be seen what remains of the **'Old Dean Road'**. It has been cleaned and cleared by members of the Local History Society. Doubts have been cast about the origins of this ancient road. A deal of local controversy has been roused. Indigenous Foresters, who have long memories and a wealth of tales and legend, insist that it is indeed a Roman road. Prestigious writers, and writers of guide books, over the years have referred to this road as being Roman, but some have a different opinion. **A.W. Trotter** wrote a fascinating book called the 'The

Dean Road', in which he traced the road from Lydney through Soudley and Littledean to Mitcheldean. It then disappears, possibly in the direction of Ariconium, a Roman industrial settlement near Ross On Wye. **The Dean Archaeological Group** have suggested that it is of Roman origin, but the debate still continues locally.

Dean Road

This scenic road leads to **Soudley.** The name means a self clearing and that is just what Soudley is, a clearing made in the forest land. Soudley is the home of the **Dean Heritage Museum.** All visitors to the area should make the effort to pay a visit to this museum. It is an extremely well run place. Here much of the Dean's heritage is preserved and there are fascinating artefacts, most pertaining to life as it once was, in the Forest of Dean. All are well displayed and presented.

The museum is also the centre for many activities. Walks on nature trails through the surrounding woodlands are arranged touching on things of natural and historical interest. **Charcoal burning** is often demonstrated. Children are well catered for, with the splendid adventure play area as well as an assortment of living creatures to observe. The museum also hosts such things as art exhibitions and other things of cultural interest. There are some excellent craft shops based at the museum, as well as the **Heritage Kitchen** which looks after the 'inner man' and which, by prior arrangement, can cater for parties. Near the museum, one of the **Soudley Ponds** lies in a deep valley and affords a favourite area for walking. In the area of Soudley at the site of the other Soudley Pond there is a circular tour through the woodlands which can be taken by car. This is called **Blaize Bailey.** The route leads to the very top of the valley in which the ponds lie and from the top the Forestry Commission have cleared certain areas as viewpoints.

This area is particularly lovely in the springtime when the woodlands are carpeted with bluebells and the beech trees have the first blush of new leaves showing. In the woods between the road and the ponds are grown some of the tallest trees in Western Europe. They are grown to provide the masts for the tall ships which often come to Gloucester docks for necessary repairs.

These places are all close to a T junction near the converted Methodist Church on the B4431. At the junction a left turn can be taken in the direction of Parkend. To the right of this road, set back from the main road, is a row of houses. They are called **The Barracks.** How they got this rather unusual name is not known, but it is recalled that about in 1912 there were soldiers stationed here. The name could have come from that time.

Turning to the right just beyond the Barracks is the **New Fancy Viewpoint** and picnic site. This area was made on the site of one of the Dean's larger collieries. There is a path to the top of the viewpoint, which was once the colliery slag heap. It is well worth the effort needed to climb to the top. From this vantage point, walled for safety because there are potentially dangerous steep drops around, a large area of the surrounding forest can be seen. As with all the Forestry Commission picnic sites there are toilet and other facilities here.

Travelling on the road which leads from New Fancy Viewpoint in the direction of Speech House, the area of the forest on the left is known as the **Saintlow Enclosure.** This area of forest probably contains some of the most remote woodlands in the Dean. It is bounded on the north by the

B4226 which runs in front of the Speech House.

During the 1939/45 war this part of the forest was used as a vast, and naturally camouflaged, ammunition store. The woodland to the left of this forest road is **Russell's Inclosure.** The road between New Fancy Viewpoint and the Speech House is the eastern boundary for Russell's Inclosure. To the north is the B4234. This makes it possible to drive round the perimeter of this large inclosure.

Russell's Inclosure is truly the heart of the Forest. It is one of the Dean's most prestigious areas of woodland. In 1993 the Forest Enterprise, Forest of Dean, received an Award of Excellence for this particular part of the Forest.

This inclosure encompasses many things of interest. On the east side the B4234 passes the **Cannop Ponds** in the valley of that name. Close beside the ponds are all that remains of the railway track which once went through the woodland to Lydney.

Where the B4228 and the B4234 meet at Cannop crossroads was the site of the last commercial charcoal works in the Dean.

Some of the inclosure is a part of the **Cannop Valley Nature Reserve.** The south west of the inclosure is also a part of the

Nagshead Nature Reserve. This includes an area of Special Scientific interest. At the beginning of the twentieth century Russell's Inclosure had a predominance of oak trees. In the north-east corner of Russell's Inclosure can be seen some of the oldest oaks in the Forest. They were planted in 1720.

Today there are different species of trees growing in the inclosure. Care is taken with the planting and nurturing of these trees. Conservation is also a major consideration and the growth has been cleared from the immediate edges of some of the rides. This is to encourage butterflies and great care is taken to preserve and nurture wild life. About half-way along this road between New Fancy Viewpoint towards Speech House, on the left is a turning into the wood with a small parking area. A sign indicates that this is **Boys Grave**.

Many years ago the gipsies, who frequented the Forest, would often camp at this site because close by is a natural spring. The gipsies would make clothes pegs which they sold at the cottages around the place. One of the little gypsy boys was busily employed cutting wood to make the pegs when his knife slipped and so badly cut his wrist that he bled to death before any assistance could be given. He was buried at the spot. From that day the gipsies never came back to this camping ground. The little boy is immortalised in that today the place bears the name Boys Grave.

When passing through this area at dawn or dusk, it is well to keep an eye open for a glimpse of the **fallow deer** which belong to the herd which frequents this part of the Forest. Provision is made for their care by the Rangers who are on the staff of the Forest Enterprise. There are actually two herds of deer in the Forest of Dean. One of the herds is in the Highmeadow Woods which stretch from beyond Monmouth to Staunton. The other is the Speech House herd.

Speech House stands at the junction of the B4226 and the road from the New Fancy. The B4226, which passes in front of the Speech House, is marked on some of the old maps as a Roman road. It would be right to say that several of the roads through the Forest are similarly made on what was originally a Roman way. Today the Speech House, which belongs to the Forestry Commission, is leased to the hotel chain of Trusthouse Forte. It stands in the very centre of the Forest of Dean and is a hotel of great character.

The Verderers of the Forest of Dean hold their meetings at the Speech House. They are officially charged with looking after the vert (plants) and the venison (game) of the Forest. This court of the

Verderers dates from the twelfth century. Sadly, today the powers of the Verderers are minimal but they do work in close conjunction with the senior staff from Forest Enterprise who manage the Dean with a great deal of care and expertise.

The Verderers are elected on the authority of a writ of the Crown when a vacancy occurs. This is a rare occurence because a Verderer is elected for life. An election is arranged by the High Sheriff of the County. At the present time these elections are held at the Shire Hall in Gloucester. The electoral procedure is done with a show of hands. Only freeholders are

Speech House

allowed to vote. Any expenses incurred are borne by those putting themselves up for election. The Court of Verderers is convened every forty days. It is usually adjourned until there is sufficient business to discuss. There is no renumeration for being a Verderer. Long ago, when the post carried rather more responsibility, a Verderer did receive a buck and a doe each year. At the present time, despite the lack of any serious power it is considered to be an honour to be

a Verderer and a part of this ancient tradition. The position is treated seriously and with respect. The Verderers hold their meetings in the **old court room** of the Speech House, used generally as the dining room of the hotel.

In the year 1883 the Speech House was much enlarged. These additions were so cleverly effected that it is very difficult to distinguish the original building from the comparatively new extension. Built between 1676 and 1680 at the time when the other Crown Lodges were built in the Forest, the Speech House has often been a haven for travellers, standing as it does in the heart of the woodlands.

When the mines were working in the Forest, for many years, on the first Saturday in July, the miners held a demonstration in the field adjoining the Speech House. It was a tremendous occasion, and one which is still remembered by the older generation in Dean. Today, as well as the Verderers, the Freeminers and sometimes the Commoners hold their meetings at the Speech House.

The Speech House is famous for its poster beds. They are still an enviable feature of the hotel. These beds were made in 1840 for the home of one of the Dean's most powerful and wealthy mine-owners. When this man's mansion home and furniture was sold in 1895, the Speech House acquired the beds as well as some fine chairs which bore the crest of the family who had owned them. They now stand in the courtroom on the platform and are used by the Verderers.

The whole ambience of the Speech House is one of mellow restfulness. The past has left its mark, for so much of Dean's history has been made here. It has been visited by many people over the years. The visitors include the Queen and the Duke of Edinburgh who came to the Speech House in

1957. They both planted an oak tree near the Speech House. The two spades were inscribed and now hang in the Verderer's courtroom, which is usually the hotel dining room.

Although many tales are told of times long gone when the Forest was a very different place to the one we know, today the Speech House has taken on a much more peaceful role. It provides a haven for those wishing to escape from the rigours and the rush of this present day life. In the summer time, when the bracken fern stands as tall as a man amongst the mighty oaks, there is nothing to break the spell of peace and tranquillity around the Speech House, except the sound of willow leather as cricket is played on in the field alongside the hotel.

Immediately opposite the Speech House there stands a stone pillar which traditionally marks the centre of the Forest. There is an inscription upon it which states:-

This stone
which by tradition
marks the centre of the Forest
was replaced to mark
the 90th. birthday
of Viscount Bledisloe, PG, GCMG, KBE.
as a Verderer
September 21st. 1957

At the back of the Speech House, through the woodlands, is what remains of the once famous **Spruce Drive.** This stretches into the depths of the forest for some miles. The trees were cut down because they were attacked by some spruce beetle. There is still the wide path leading into the forest but now without the spruce which gives the path its name. Some distance down this ride is a lake. This area is very popular with walkers. There are very good car parking facilities.

Near the Spruce Ride is the **Dean Hall School**. It is an interesting building which blends in well with the surrounding woodland. At one time this belonged to the Forestry Commission and was used by them for training purposes. Now it is a special needs school.

To the south of the Speech House is the **Arboretum**. Like many of the forest's picnic sites the Arboretum is suitable for wheelchairs. This is a very pleasant and restful place to spend time. There are seats at certain points to enable the visitor to contemplate the beauty of this place. There are a good collection of trees in the Arboretum, both broadleaf and conifer, many from other countries and many that are quite rare. This small Arboretum is a great asset to the Forest of Dean and it provides easy walking for those who find difficulty managing hilly terrain.

Around the area of the Arboretum can be seen the holly trees of **Holly Wood**. These trees were planted as food for the deer. This area, the heart of the Forest, is where the woodlands are at their best. It is here that some of the finest and oldest oak trees are growing. In the unfenced area opposite the Speech House, to the north-east of Russell's Inclosure, are some fine oak trees. Until the nineteenth century oak trees had been grown in the Dean to supply the naval dockyards which were very important customers.

At the time of the 1914/18 War the Forest of Dean was a place of mostly hardwoods, with a predominance of oak trees. A great deal of felling was done to meet the demands of those unsettled times. In 1924 the Forest of Dean was put under the management of the Forestry Commission. There was an intention then to plant conifers to replace the trees which had been felled. Following the Second World War, when more of the remaining hardwoods were felled, even more were planted. Today the balance of hardwoods and softwoods in the Forest of Dean is carefully maintained.

The Forest of Dean is expertly and carefully managed. Careful harvesting and re-afforestation is carried out. Picnic sites and waymarked paths set out with imagination and a lot of thought. The Forest of Dean is the ideal place for those who seek to enjoy the things of nature.

From the Speech House it is a short distance down the hill on the B4326 to the **Beechenhurst** Lodge and picnic site. This picnic and recreation area is a very popular spot for visitors and locals who wish to spend some time in the Forest. It has been made on one of the old colliery sites and has been completely reorganised with new parking areas, many of them in bays set in the woodland. There is also a one way system. A charge is now made for parking.

The focal point of this site is the splendid lodge opened in 1992 by the Duchess of Kent. This lodge, which is open all year round, has a shop where souvenirs can be bought as well as trail guides, leaflets and maps. Refreshments are also sold and there are excellent toilet facilities. Outside there is a play area for children which is very popular.

Above the Lodge is a meeting room, with easy access for everyone by way of a gently sloping wooden walkway.

In 1993 Forest Enterprise was presented with an Award of Excellence for Beechenhurst picnic site and lodge as well as for Russell's Inclosure.

These prestigious awards are given by the Forestry Commission to projects in the public and private sector of Forestry.

Beechenhurst is an extremely pleasant place with views over the surrounding woodlands. It is the starting point for many leisure activities. There are walks through the woodlands, including **Russell's Inclosure** which is the opposite side of the main road B4224 to Beechenhurst. Self guide leaflets to Russell's Inclosure can be bought at the Lodge shop. They contain many things of interest about the area of the Forest including the fact that it was named afterVivian de Russelhalle who was a woodward in the Forest in 1270.

Beechenhurst is also the start of the **Sculpture Trail**. This covers about four miles of well marked trail. These sculptures are now a very popular and much visited feature of the Forest of Dean. Set as they are in the central woodlands they take those who follow the trail through some of the loveliest areas of the Forest. There are also some sculptures on the Beechenhurst site. From Beechenhurst it is easy to explore the Cannop Nature Reserve which stretches through the woodlands along the Valley.

Visits can be also be made from here to **'Speculation'** another converted colliery site. The site takes its name from the colliery which was there . This reflects the highly imaginative and often thought provoking names which were used to identify some of these old mines.

At the old **Cannop colliery site,** well within striking distance of Beechenhurst, bicycles can be hired from **Pedalabikeaway.**

Forest Enterprise hope that in the future more and more use will be made of cycling facilities in the forest. They are already involved in a scheme to convert some of the old railway and tramway tracks into cycling tracks, in an endeavour to encourage cyclists to explore the forest this way.

Cannop Ponds, also in this area, has excellent parking facilities for visitors. Fishing is allowed on the ponds. The fishing rights belong to a local syndicate and a licence for this can be obtained from sports shops. Walkers are very welcome in the Forest of Dean. It is a place where walking is the best way of seeing and appreciating the unspoilt beauty of this ancient forest.

St. Briavels to Coleford

Route two - through the forest is on the B4228 in the direction of **Coleford.** Beyond the first bend on this pleasant road is **Bearse Farm.** This extends on either side of the road. Just beyond the the farm is the **Bearse Common.** Theoretically both these places

belong to Bream. This area of the Bearse has provided local archaeologists with evidence that the place was known to Neolithic man.

At **Trow Green,** where the road from Bream joins the B4228, there is another of the delightful toll houses which were once so much a part of the life of the Forest of Dean. The house is single storey as were all the original toll houses. At this point there is a turning on to the B4231 which is signposted **Clearwell.** Some distance along this road is the ancient village of Clearwell, known in years gone by as Wellington and then Clowerwell. Entering the village, on the left is the **castle.** The entrance to the castle is impressive and leads to a short tree lined drive. Even though it bears the distinguished name it is not, in the strictest sense of the word, a castle. Indeed it is of Gothic revival architecture. The place where the castle now stands was thought to have been the site of a Roman villa. The earliest records tell of an estate here belonging to Crusader Sir John Joce or Joyce. This building was replaced by an Elizabethan mansion. Part of this mansion house was incorporated into the present building which was erected in 1727 for the **Wyndham family.**

From 1810 until her death in 1870 **Caroline Countess of Dunraven** lived at the castle having inherited it from the Wyndham family. She was a most a generous benefactress to the village of Clearwell.

As well as making great improvements to her home, Caroline Countess of Dunraven caused the present church to be built at Clearwell. It is the next building past the castle entrance. The church is built in French Gothic style of the 13th century. It is constructed of local red sandstone with Bath stone dressing. It was consecrated on 5th April 1866 and dedicated to St. Peter.

Many things in Clearwell demonstrate the generosity of the Countess of Dunraven. The school was one of her projects as was the **village hall**, which never seemed to be quite finished. On the roadside before reaching the castle, and on the opposite side of the road, are two charming houses. The largest of the two bears the name of **Dunraven**. It is said that in the 1860s Caroline Countess of Dunraven had this building erected to serve as a hospital for the village people. Sadly there is no record of there ever having been more than one patient in this hospital. That was one of the workmen employed on the building who fell and broke his leg. The other house alongside Dunraven is called **Baynham**. This house has obviously been enlarged with stone left over from the building of the church since the distinctive

red stone used in the building of the church can be recognised in both these houses.

The last private resident to live in the castle before it was badly damaged was **Colonel Charles Granville Vereker.** He was a cousin to Lord Gort who commanded the forces of the B.E.F. in the early years of the 1939-45 war. In 1929 the castle was almost destroyed by fire and many valuable and precious contents were lost. Colonel Vereker then set about enlarging and completely renovating Baynham and that is where he made his home for the rest of his life.

Frank Yates, the son of a gardener at the castle, lived his childhood days in the lodge of the castle. He had a great affection for the big house. Some years after the fire, Yates, by then a business man in Blackpool, chanced to hear that the castle was falling into a serious state of dilapidation. He made the decision that he would come back to his roots. He bought the castle and with his wife and family lived in the grounds in a caravan whilst they set about the mammoth task of virtually rebuilding the place. Today the castle is used as a hotel.

The centre of the crossroads in Clearwell is marked by a fine **14th century stone cross** in early Gothic style. Some previous, unsympathetic, repairs to the cross were rectified in the middle of the 19th century at the expense of the Countess of Dunraven.

Clearwell has a famous son, **Private Francis George (Chris) Miles** who on October 23rd 1918 won the V.C. for outstanding gallantry. He was the first man in Gloucestershire to be awarded such a medal. In recognition of the honour which Private Miles brought to Gloucestershire and to his village, two rows of cottages in Clearwell were named **Miles Cottages**. George Miles died in 1961.

Previously known as Wellington as well as Clowerwell the present day name of Clearwell came from a spring of clear, pure water. This spring supplied the settlement which grew up around this source of water which was never known to fail even in the driest summers.

The Wyndham Arms, standing near the crossroads, is today a hostelry of excellent repute. It was thought for some time to have been the home of Sir John Joce or Joyce who was buried in the graveyard at nearby by Newland church in the year 1349. **The Butchers Arms** in Clearwell is also a house of some age and character.

Continue on the B4321 to **Newland.** This village is without doubt one of the most ancient of forest settlements and has played an important part in the life of Dean in that the **Church of Newland** was for many years considered to be the church which served the whole of the Forest of Dean.

On the approach road to Newland the village can be seen rising from the valley through which we are approaching. The church is the dominant building set against a backdrop of tree topped fields.

Newland is a pretty village. It acquired its name because it was land taken from the surrounding forest - New Land. Many of the houses in Newland are houses of some size which is quite unusual in forest villages. As would be expected, the church is the heart and centre of this village. It is unofficially known as 'The Cathedral of the Forest' and, for such a modest village, it is indeed a large church. It was built by the first Rector, Robert Wakering, in the early part of the 13th century. The next incumbent at Newland was to become Archbishop of York. The church is **All Saints Church**. It houses the small Greyndour brass of the Forest Freeminer. This is said to depict the fact that, because of his unique privileges, the freeminer of the Forest of Dean is more important than the Knight.

Once outside in the graveyard, now kept inside the church, is the effigy of Jenkin Wyrall, Forester of Fee. His dog, no doubt in life his constant companion, is also a part of the carved effigy. There are other interesting monuments and artefacts within the church.

Within the churchyard of Newland Church is the **village cross**. This is at least 600 years old but it has a comparatively new shaft. The very attractive almshouses which stand beside the boundary of the church were founded by William Jones. A local boy, legend tells us that Jones was so poor that when he went to Monmouth to have his shoes repaired he took them and did not pay for the repairs. He then went to London to seek fame and fortune. Having done just that, William Jones did settle his debts for the repair of his shoes. He also did a great deal for the place where he had grown up.

Newland had rows of almshouses on each side of the churchyard. The one row and the building that once housed the first **Bell's Grammar School** were founded by Edward Bell in 1623. The row of sixteen almhouses standing beside the road which is on the opposite side of the churchyard were founded by William Jones. He also provided the superior **Lecturer's House** which stands beside the row of almshouses. His generosity is recorded on a tablet set on the almshouses which reads:-

These Almshouses for eight men & eight women Parishioners of Newland and the habitation adjoining for a Lecturer, were founded A.D. 1615 by Mr. William Jones Citizen and Haberdasher of London and he appointed the Worshipful Company of Haberdashers Governors.

There is also another inscribed tablet to say that these Almshouses were modernised in 1954 by the Worshipful Company of Haberdashers - Governors of the William Jones Charity.

William Jones was instrumental in the founding of the Haberdashers Monmouth Boys School, and in 1892 the Monmouth Girls School was also founded by the Worshipful Company of Haberdashers.

The village hostelry, which stands opposite the main church gate, is an interesting building which dates from the 13th century.

For some reason this inn set deep in the heart of rural Gloucestershire bears the strange name of **The Ostrich.**

Perhaps the inn's unusual name can be partly explained by the crest which is at the **Dower House.** This is an ostrich head with a key in its mouth. This Dower House was built in the 18th century by Squire Probyn.

Newland is a place of large houses and is now a very desirable place to live. In the heart of rural countryside it is a village of great character and history.

Return to Clearwell and at the village cross follow the road signposted **Clearwell Caves and Iron Mine**. A short distance up this country road out of Clearwell the mine can be seen on the right. Just beyond the mine there is a sign which directs to the mine car park.

This place is one of the most popular tourist attractions in the area. A visit to the Clearwell Caves is usually on the itinerary of all visitors to the area. The mining of iron was one of the major industries in the Forest of Dean for many hundreds of years. The Clearwell iron mines are rather different from the accepted idea of mining for they are in fact natural caves. The iron, which was mined here, was water deposited over a period of many hundreds of years.

There has been evidence found to show that these iron mine caves were known to the Romans. Since that time they were worked for hundreds of years by men of the locality. At Clearwell the iron mining industry began to decline at the beginning of the twentieth century. It briefly revived during the years of the First and Second World Wars.

For the more recent years that the Clearwell iron mines were working, the colour works at **Milkwall** was also in production. There the ochre obtained as a by-product of the iron ore was made into a colouring agent.

In 1968, the then disused Clearwell iron mine caves were taken over by a local man, Mr. Ray Wright. He opened them to the public and instigated further exploration of the underground mining complex. Most of the caves are Clearwell are at a depth of about one hundred feet. The further exploration has made possible the opening up of workings at an even greater depth. It is advised that only those who are quite fit attempt to go to the lower levels.

Much has been done at the Clearwell caves to make it of interest to those visiting. There is a small museum, a gift shop and a restaurant where snacks, drinks and light meals are available.

Mr. Wright, who has done much to help recall the days of iron mining in the Forest, is also a Verderer of the Forest of Dean.

From Clearwell Caves it is a short distance to the junction with the B4228 St. Briavels - Coleford road. At this junction, turn right in the direction of St. Briavels. A few yards along this road to the left is the **Lambsquay picnic site.** Just behind the sign which indicates this fact is the rather worn and strangely shaped **Gattle Stone**. It stands on what is known as **Clearwell Meend** despite the fact that it is on the opposite side of the road from the common land which is above Clearwell Caves.

Many theories have been put forward about the reason for, and the origin of, this stone. This area has been the site of much iron mining activity, not only at Clearwell Caves but much nearer, in the immediate vicinity of the **Lambsquay Hotel** near the road junction. It is interesting to note that this hotel was built on the site of the old **Lambsquay iron mines.**

It is an ancient iron mining site and one of many of the mines in this locality which were working even before the Romans came to Britain.

Because of the proximity of these iron workings, the name Gattle could possibly be derived from the ancient word gat which refers to channels or passages in the ground. There are an abundance of these near this place.

This stone was known for many years as **Eleanor's Stone**. It was said that Queen Eleanor, on her way from Wales, paid a guide ninepence to take her through the forest. When she got to this particular spot this is where she sat and rested.

Return to the road junction on the St. Briavels - Coleford B4228 road. Here take the right turn alongside the garden centre. Milkwall is a suburb of Coleford. It is in fact only separated from that town by the industry which developed on the designated site at the edge of the town of Coleford.

Although to the casual observer **Milkwall** seems a quiet place it was once served by the **railway**. The line which linked Coleford to Lydney passed through Milkwall. This railway, which for so many years provided a very essential link between the Forest and the outside world is remembered in Coleford where the old waiting room has been converted into a small museum of memorabilia of those times.

There is, near the road junction in Milkwall, a road leading to the right and signposted **Ellwood**. This leads to another small forest settlement. Near Ellwood, in the woodlands can be found the remains of works which once belonged to the **Mushet family**. It could be said that the Father, David Mushet, was the forerunner of the nineteenth century industrial revolution in the Forest of Dean.

The Forest of Dean District Council realised some years ago that the remains of the Mushet works are of some industrial archaeological interest. So they arranged to have capped what remained of the walls and they generally tidied up the site. The great grinding stone can be seen lying amongst the remains of this once important works.

Retracing steps to the junction with the B4228 near the Lambsquay Hotel a right turning on to the road finds at a short distance down this B4228 an entrance, on the left, which leads to **Puzzle Wood** at **Perrygrove Farm**. These are, like the Scowles at Bream, old open iron workings. They were used at the time of the Roman occupation but were most probably worked even before then. This place is well worth taking time to explore. The woodlands in which the Scowles are contained have been laid out with walks and is in a spectacular setting. It takes the name of Puzzle from the fact that once having entered the place it is often very difficult to find a way back out again.

Coleford can be reached by continuing on the B4228 road from which can be seen, on the left, the Smithkline Beecham factory.

COLEFORD

Gloucester - 19 miles
Tourist Information -
27 Market Place.
tel: 0594 836307
Campsites - ref. Forest Enterprise, Campsite Office, (Dept. A.), Christchurch, Nr Coleford.

See Gazetteer for leisure and recreational facilities

This Forest town of **Coleford** takes its name from Charcoal Ford reflecting the time when the burning of charcoal was an important industry in this locality.

Around this place in past ages the traditional industries of the area, such as coal and iron mining and stone quarrying was carried out. All that is now past. Coleford reflects the present day with shopping facilities, provision for recreational pursuits and a pleasant, open aspect. Today Coleford is the administrative centre of the Forest of Dean. The **Council Offices**, built to centralise the administrative functions of the Forest of Dean District Council, are based here. Forest Enterprise, which looks after the interests of the **Forestry Commission** in Dean, is based at the **Crown Offices** in Coleford. Working from the Crown offices is

Coleford

the **Deputy Gaveller**. He holds a post which is both ancient and unique. The Forest of Dean is the only place in the world to have the services of a Gaveller.

Because of the peculiarity of the mineral rights in the Forest of Dean in which, by ancient custom, the Monarch had a share, a Gaveller came to the Dean to protect the Monarch's rights. So it was that, in the years now long gone, the Gaveller would call at the small mines, of which there was a plethora in the Forest. He called on Tuesdays between 'Mattens and Masse' to collect the 'King's Penny' from each miner working in the mine.

Now the Deputy Gaveller works in conjunction with the Forestry Authorities and is responsible to the Commissioners. He arranges the letting of mines to the few existing free-miners who still claim this ancient privilege. The Crown has always maintained the ownership of mine sites, so the Deputy Gaveller has to make the necessary arrangements and see that all conditions are observed and adhered to. He also collects any royalties on any mineral be it iron, stone or coal which is mined, or dug, from beneath the earth of the Forest of Dean.

Although modern in outlook, Coleford has a long history. It dates back to before the Roman invasion. There are indications that it was inhabited in the Bronze Age. Some years ago, in a garden at **Coombs Park**, two flint knives and an arrow head dating from the Bronze Age were discovered during building operations and it is possible that a burial place on the site was being disturbed. The excavations which were carried out by the **Dean Archaeological Group** at High Nash proved that Coleford was known to the Romans.

The activities of the **Civil War** touched, and affected, Coleford. There was a serious skirmish in the town on the 20th February 1643 when a contingent of some 500 horse and 1500 foot soldiers from the Royalist Army marched into Coleford on their way from Monmouth to Gloucester. In the centre of Coleford they were stopped by a troop of Parliamentarian soldiers and a large number of local country people. Major General Sir Richard Lawley, the Commander of the foot soldiers, was shot. The bullet, a silver one, was fired from a window of the **Angel Hotel**. There was no other fatality recorded from this confrontation. In the fracas of this skirmish the **Market House** in the centre of the town was burnt down.

After the Civil War, Charles II made a generous contribution of £50 towards the building of a new **Town Hall** in Coleford.

One of the most interesting houses in Coleford is **Poolway House** which was a sixteenth century manor house and is now an excellent hotel and restaurant. Legend says that **Charles I** was given shelter at this manor house during the Civil War. When the Civil War ended, as an acknowledgement of this help, Charles II granted to the owner of the Poolway House certain privileges.

For many years Coleford had no established church. In 1821 an

Anglican chapel was built in the centre of the town. All that now remains of that church is the tower which still marks the centre of the town. Close to the tower is a **stone cross** which was raised on the exact spot where once the altar of the church stood.

The bell in the tower of the old church was last rung in honour of **Captain Angus Buchanan**, V.C. Captain Angus Buchanan was the son of a Coleford doctor. He was awarded the V.C. when, in the 1914-18 war, with great heroism, he rescued two wounded comrades. He himself was wounded three times and as a result lost his sight. When the war ended, Captain Buchanan went to Oxford to study law. Then he returned to Coleford and practiced as a solicitor.

A committee was set up in Coleford to administer funds which had been raised to provide some sort of permanent recognition of Captain Buchanan's bravery. When consulted about what form this should take Captain Buchanan answered 'Somewhere for the young children to play'. It was then that the **Angus Buchanan Recreation Field** was purchased and developed as a place for children to play. The iron entrance gates to the recreation field were specially made. They incorporate the V.C. and the date of the heroic incident.

Captain Angus Buchanan lived the rest of his life in Coleford and that is where he died. He was buried, with all honour, in Coleford Cemetery which is next to the playing field.

The original Anglican Church, which stood in the centre of Coleford, was demolished because it was not big enough to accommodate the congregations. It was not possible to enlarge the church because the land around it belonged to the Market Company who would not sell so a new site was found. The new church was built in a prominent position on **Bowen's Hill.** It is a landmark in the town. The church was opened in 1880 and was dedicated to **St. John.** Perhaps because of the lack of an early established church, Coleford was to become the unofficial centre of non-conformism in the Forest.

In 1698 a Presbyterian meeting house was built in Coleford. It was said to be the only such place between Gloucester and Abergavenny. A year later, a Friends meeting house was built. The **Reverend John Wesley** knew Coleford. He visited the place twice, once in 1756 and again in 1763.

The Baptist movement in the Forest of Dean seems to have emanated from Coleford. Small wonder that John Wesley found the people confused by disputations.

In 1799, in Coleford, was born Mary Botham. She later married William Howitt. Together they wrote delightful stories for children. Even though **Mary Howitt** moved away from Coleford she has always been remembered there for her literary work.

Coleford was the place where the industrial revolution of the nineteenth century began in the Forest. It began with David Mushet, a truly brilliant metallurgist. He made his home at a house known as Forest House then called Tump House. He had three sons. One of the sons, Robert Forester Mushet, working in a shed not far from Tump House in 1856, perfected the process of self hardening steel which was to be known as the **Bessemer Process**. Evidence of this famous family can still be found in Coleford today for they are remembered in place names.

Dame Edna Healey, wife of the once prominent Labour politician Denis Healey, was born and brought up in the town of Coleford and continues to visit and maintain an interest in local affairs.

With the decline in the iron industry, then later the closing of the coal mines, Coleford has found a new role. Small industries have grown up. Coleford is indeed fortunate in that it has one major industry which provides a great deal of employment in the area. It is the factory of **Smithkline Beecham**. In 1946 a factory was started on this site and was affectionately regarded and known by its name of Carters. It was here that the world renowned blackcurrant drink, Ribena, was first perfected and produced.

Future and indeed present day historians have reason to be grateful for the research and writings of Dr. C.E. Hart, a Coleford man. Dr. Hart has written in great detail and accuracy on many aspects of past and present life in the Forest of Dean. His works are invaluable and will provide, for future generations, an excellent record of the history of the Forest of Dean. At the time of writing Dr. C.E. Hart is the Senior Verderer of the Forest.

Coleford has been subjected to a great deal of development. Even so its long history has not been lost. Old and new has blended quite happily together and Coleford has adapted quite easily to the demands of this age.

Leaving Coleford on the B4028, at the first crossroads turn left on to the B4432. This leads in the direction of Berry Hill.

The widespread area of **Berry Hill** is a typical forest settlement. It grew from the need for houses for the miners who worked in the local pits, and their families. The original cottages have nearly all been renovated and greatly improved. New houses have been built and employment is no longer found in the pits but in rather more salubrious conditions.

This is the village where the famous playwright **Dennis Potter** was born and brought up as the son of a miner. Life in this place, and indeed in the Forest generally,

was very different years ago. It was this place, and the way things were, which provided material for some of Dennis Potter's writings. Berry Hill merges almost imperceptively with **Christchurch**.

If Berry Hill and Christchurch are visited, the route continues on the A4136 from the Five Acres crossroads, in the direction of Gloucester, which is signposted.

This road passes the **Lakers Comprehensive School** and the **Royal Forest of Dean College**, on the left. Each side of this main road is bounded by mature woodland with a predominance of beech trees.

The small hamlet of **Edge End** is on either side of this road. There is evidence to be seen here of the one time coal mining industry.

From the cleared area to the left there are extensive views over the Brecon Beacons and the Black Mountains of Wales.

In the woodlands, a short distance beyond the hamlet of **Edge End**, is the **picnic site** of that name. It is well signposted by the Forestry Commission. This picnic site is an excellent place to stop a while with facilities for picnics and toilets. It is set in a pleasant area of woodland. The site also provides a wonderful viewpoint.

The A4136 continues through undulating countryside. The road passes along the edge of the village of **Worrall Hill**. At the bottom of a steep hill there is a crossroads. The road to the left leads to **Lydbrook**, to the right the B4234 road leads into the woodlands of the **Cannop Valley Nature Reserve**. The Forestry Commission have designated it a nature reserve, and at all times of the year it is full of the wonders of nature. **Deer** can often be glimpsed and the bird life is very interesting. The trees, predominantly oak, are interspersed with beech, scotch pine, and other varieties. The valley which reaches to Parkend has to be explored to be appreciated for it is a microcosm of the whole Forest of Dean.

In this valley is the **Speculation picnic area**. Again an old colliery site has been used to provide recreational facilities for this day and age. The name is indicative of the risks which were taken by those who mined in the Forest. A few yards beyond Speculation there is a track which leads to the iron road, one of the sculptures on the trail from **Beechenhurst**.

At this point, to the left, the **Cannop Valley brook** can be seen flowing through the woodland providing some excellent picnic spots on its banks. The water from the brook flows into a pond which was made, in 1936, to take the outflow of the, often very warm, water from the Cannop colliery. This pond is a favourite place for model boat enthusiasts.

The site of the now defunct **Cannop colliery** is on the opposite side of the road. Its primary use now is as a depot for the local council roads division. Cannop Colliery was sunk in 1908. It was a relatively modern colliery. It was sunk to the lowest levels of the Forest of Dean coal basin. There were serious problems with water which were all very well dealt with, in that there was never any serious accident in this pit through flooding. Water was a common problem in all the Forest of Dean collieries but particularly so at Cannop. There was no gas in Forest mines so the miners were able to use the open carbide lamps for lighting. They just had to contend with the difficulties allied with excess water which needed constant and costly pumping operations.

The B4234 continues to the Cannop crossroads. On the left the road passes two rows of cottages built in 1912 to accommodate key workers from the Cannop colliery. At the crossroads there is a garden centre where the plants and other items sold are displayed in the lovely setting of this bit of Forest land.

It was here on the other side of the B4226 that the very last charcoal works, the **Cannop Distillation Works**, stood.

The B4234 goes straight across this often busy crossroads to pass, on the right, the two Cannop ponds. Beyond the Cannop Ponds the B4234 passes the **Forest of Dean Stone Works** before reaching Parkend.

Returning to the point of diversion at **Mirey Stock** crossroads where the A4136 is crossed by the B4234, continue on the B4136 in the direction of Mitcheldean and Gloucester.

Carrying on along the A4136, the road approaches another small hamlet, Brierley. The stretch of woodlands on the right have the unusual name of God's Great Meadow.

The houses in it do not intrude into the woodland on the right. This small place is where **Winifred Foley** was born. She lived here for the early years of her life before leaving the Forest of Dean to live in London. Winifred Foley is well known for her book 'A Child in the Forest' and various sequels. Copies are readily available in local bookshops.

Up the hill behind the village of Brierley is a woodland road which leads to the school which Winifred

Foley writes about in her 'Child in the Forest'. The woods around this place were well known to her in her childhood.

Close to this quiet little hamlet, away in the woods opposite the service garage and houses of the settlement, is the site of what was once one of the Dean's most prestigious mines. A well defined track leads out of the hamlet to this place. It was the **Trafalgar mine**. It was owned and managed locally and employed a large number of men. At one time last century a thousand men were employed in this one pit. The Trafalgar pit was the first mine in the Forest of Dean to have a strike. This took place in 1874. The men who managed and were shareholders in this pit were pioneers in the field of electricity. They conducted many experiments with this form of lighting and the Trafalgar pit was the first colliery in the world to use the power of electricity for blasting.

Leaving Brierley the A4136 continues through woodland. A short distance from Brierley on the right of the road there is a concrete erection at the side of the road. This mundane and unimaginative edifice hides a well.

Many years ago when the Forest was a wild, and often dangerous place, those who travelled through the Forest often did so in fear and trepidation. After leaving Mitcheldean, no doubt the traveller would be in some haste to arrive at Coleford, and relative safety. The same would apply to travellers leaving Coleford to come in the other direction. When the tired and weary traveller reached this spot, just outside present day Brierley, he was always grateful to 'Stay and Drink' at the well beside the roadway. To this day that well and the area round it is still known by that name.

On this road also can be seen one of the old Forest Lodges which were built in the late seventeenth century. Standing to the left on rising land at some distance from the roadway, and in its own grounds, is Herbert Lodge where once the Crown Keeper in charge of the **Ruardean Walk** lived. Today it is privately owned.

The hill on which **Herbert Lodge** is built gradually continues to rise to the summit. This is the top of **Ruardean Hill,** the highest point in the Forest of Dean rising 951 feet above sea level. It is said that here all the winds of heaven meet.

On a clear day there are very extensive views towards the Malvern Hills, the Brecon Beacons, the Black Mountains and it is claimed that **nine counties** can be seen and the view extends as far as **Plynlimmon** on the heights

of which Severn and Wye rise within half a mile of each other.

Just outside the entrance gates to Herbert Lodge stands one of the old milestones. This tells those who care to look that the distance to London is 119 miles.

On the right of the highway is a vast mound now tree covered. It can easily be identified as a colliery slag heap. The remains of the disused colliery is here. This was the **Northern United Colliery**.

After the depression of the 1920-30's when unemployment was rife in the Forest of Dean, the government of the day gave some assistance towards the sinking of a pit which it was hoped would provide work and help relieve some of the poverty in the area.

This pit was sunk by the **Crawshay Company**. In May 1933 the first sod was cut and work on sinking this pit began. It was in fact the last large commercial pit to be sunk in the Forest. It was also the last to close. It brought the final cage full of Forest colliers to the surface on Christmas Eve 1965 and that ended a way of life that the men of the Forest had known for over 2000 years.

Men had to look for employment in other spheres. Thankfully the fast expanding factory of **Rank Xerox** in Mitcheldean willingly took into their employ the displaced miners.

The A4151 can be taken to the forest town of Cinderford. A short distance along this A4136 brings the motorist to traffic lights. Just beyond is a crossroads.

CINDERFORD

Gloucester - 14¹/₂ miles
Ross-on-Wye - 9 miles
Tourist Office - 12 Belle
                     Vue Road.
Market day - Friday
Early closing - Thursday
Library - Belle Vue Road.

See Gazetteer for leisure and recreational facilities

Cinderford is the newest of the forest towns. It is also the only town to stand within the actual forest. It came into being to fulfil a need for houses for those who came to the forest to work in the industries which flourished in this locality in the early and mid nineteenth century. Because it stands within the ancient boundary of the Forest of Dean, Cinderford is the only town where the commoner's rights apply and so sheep can often be seen wandering the streets.

Spread across an exposed hillside, Cinderford is often a very cold place. It is very much a working town. It has few buildings of any architectural note. Some of those it did have, were unfortunately sacrificed in the name of progress.

The Baptist Chapel, or as it is called today, the Baptist Church, in Cinderford is a building of some exceptional prominence and has always been a distinctive landmark in the town on account of its size and position. It was built in 1856 to help to cope with the surge of non-conformism which was sweeping through the Forest at that time. The tendency to non-conformism was much encouraged by the mine owners of that day. It was realised that hand in hand with non-conformism went temperance and a temperate workman was thought to be much more reliable than one who frequented the public houses which abounded in the area.

The main streets of Cinderford now more or less converge on the centre which is the triangle. This is made something of a focal point by the quite impressive **war memorial** which is sited here.

Once Cinderford was the unofficial centre of the Forest. Certainly it was the centre of a deal of industrial activity. Industry is still carried on in the area of Cinderford because, at the bottom end of the town, there is a well laid out and well maintained trading estate. Cinderford once had a rather splendid town hall, but sadly that has now gone. In **Belle Vue Road** stands the solid and well proportioned **St. Annal's House**. This was built in the early years of the nineteenth century. It is well built of local Forest of Dean stone. It has served many purposes and was for most of its existence a private residence. Then it was an Institute. It was vacated by the Forest of Dean District Council as a result of re-organisation and centralisation of local government. Today it belongs to the Cinderford Town Council. The Registrar of births, deaths and marriages has his office at St. Annal's House.

The first development of Cinderford began to the east. **Abbotswood**, a large tract of woodland in the area, was given to the Abbot and Monks of Flaxley Abbey by Henry III to provide timber to fire their forges down in the valley of Flaxley near the abbey. The house, which until recent years stood at Abbotswood and bore that name, was before its destruction one of the oldest houses in the locality of Cinderford. It was also the grandest residence this place has ever known. Abbotswood woodland was owned by the Crawshay family until 1994 when it reverted to the Crown. Like Abbotswood, names of certain places in Cinderford echo its

past. St. Whites, to the east, recalls that once the Cistercian, or White, monks were at Flaxley Abbey. **Flaxley Street**, in Cinderford, was so named because much of the land on to which Cinderford spread once belonged to the Flaxley Abbey estates.

Because it was a new town Cinderford did not have a church until the size of the population demanded it. Near the place where most development was taking place, the **Church of St. John** was built and dedicated in 1840. It is a typical Victorian building.

With the spread of Cinderford, another church was later built. It stands in Belle Vue Road and is dedicated to **St. Stephen**. The land on which it is built was acquired from the Flaxley Abbey estates and the first stone was laid by **Lady Crawley Boevey** from the Abbey. It has no burial ground.

Cinderford developed from the iron works which once lay all down the valley between Cinderford and the woodlands of the central Forest straddling the brook which runs through this area. This was how Cinderford got its name, from the huge cinders near the iron works and across the brook, The Cinders over the Ford.

Although not a son of Cinderford, **Leonard Clark**, a much appreciated literary figure of the twentieth century, came to Cinderford at a young age. He was brought up in the town and grew to love the Forest. Many of his poems and writings were inspired by his experience of, and his great affection for, the Forest of Dean and Cinderford.

Cinderford was also the birthplace of radio presenter **Jimmy Young**. His mother, who was for many years the organist at the Baptist Chapel, is buried in the graveyard of that place.

It could be said that Cinderford is the only place of any size which still encapsulates the nature and spirit of the true Forest amongst its indiginous inhabitants.

About a mile beyond Cinderford on A4151 is **Littledean**. A village steeped in history, it was once very much more important than the few houses which stood on the early settlement place of Cinderford known as **Littledean Woodside**.

Littledean still bears signs of its ancient origins. The streets, despite the attentions of modern day road builders, are still narrow and rather irregular. Littledean is a small place, and its name reflects this for it comes from the ancient 'Dene Parva' which means lesser or little Dean.

This place, just over the hill from the River Severn, was known to Bronze Age settlers and to the Romans. The Old Dean Roman road came through here, and in the grounds of **Littledean Hall** have been found exciting Roman remains, including what is thought to be the site of the largest Roman temple yet discovered in rural England.

Saxon remains have also been found beneath Littledean Hall, and before the Norman Conquest it was the Hall of the Lords of Dene. Through all the intervening years there has been a house standing on this site, often occupied by Verderers and senior Forest officials.

In the mid sixteenth century Littledean Hall was the home of **Richard Brayne**, Lord High Sheriff of Gloucester. This fact was denoted by the stone balls which stood on the entrance gate pillars. During the Civil War, two Royalist officers were put to the sword and killed in the dining room of Dean Hall. It is reputed to be the most haunted house in Gloucestershire. Visitors are welcome during the tourist season on payment of an entrance fee

Another very interesting house is at the other side of Littledean. It is now known as the **Red House** but it has another name '**Brayne Court**'. It was, in the sixteenth century, the home of Richard Brayne, the son of the High Sheriff who lived at Dean Hall. It is well preserved and has some Tudor panelling and mullioned windows.

Church Farm and **Dean Croft** are amongst some of Littledean's older houses.

Just on the edge of Littledean facing is what was once the **Littledean Gaol**. Now this rather forbidding building belongs to a large insurance company.

Littledean Gaol

In 1791, when gaols were rather appalling places, Sir George Onesipherous Paul was charged with the building of four Bridewells or gaols. The site he chose for one of these buildings was at Littledean. These houses of correction were models of their kind. It is said that they were the pattern for the building of Pentonville.

The Church of **St. Ethelbert** is Littledean Parish Church and stands in the village street. This church, which is mostly fourteenth century, is built on the site of a very much older building. The church is unusual in that the spire

was badly damaged in a storm in 1894. It was taken down and never rebuilt.

From the centre of Littledean, a sign can be seen directing visitors to the excellent riding facilities offered by the **Littledean Riding Stables**.

From Littledean it is about two miles to return on the A4151 through Cinderford to the Nailbridge crossroads. Travelling in the other direction from there it is about mile to the village of Ruardean.

Ruardean lies half-way up the hillside of **Ruardean Hill**. It is, from the approach road over the slight hill, a well situated village with the distinctive spire of the church rising from the midst of the surrounding buildings.

Ruardean has much in common with the other peripheral villages of Littledean and Mitcheldean, yet there is no connection whatsoever between the three places. Even the similarity in the names is purely coincidental. The name Ruardean is derived from at least seven variations on its present name. The old Celtic name Rhiw y Din, Ruworthyn meaning rough farmland, Rerewardin and River Dean are all names which have identified this place.

Not far from the church in Ruardean there was once a castellated manor house. All that now remains of this once grand building is a pile of fast disappearing stones in the field of a nearby farm.

Standing with its back to the Forest and its face towards Herefordshire, Ruardean has had close ties with that place. Until the middle of the nineteenth century, **Ruardean Church** was a chapel of ease for Walford down in the valley beside the River Wye. Then it was transferred to the Gloucester diocese.

Ruardean Church dates from 1111. One of the notable features of the church is the tympanum over the entrance door in the ancient porch. This depicts St. George slaying the dragon. It is said to be one of only four such tympanum in this country which show the saint riding his horse.

Ruardean was touched by the **Civil War**. Roundhead soldiers were garrisoned here to keep watch on the activities at Goodrich Castle down by the river. This is remembered in that the hill top immediately opposite the church was where the cannon were stationed and to this day it is known as **Shoot Hill**.

Ruardean is not a place which has to be passed through to get anywhere in particular. Even so it has played an important part in the history of the area. For many years Ruardean was subject to the **Vaughans of Courtfield** who lived across the Wye at the bottom of the steep hill. They are Lords of the **Manor of Ruardean**.

In 1641 Joan Vaughan, a widow, was jailed for hiding a priest. This was a capital offence but it is thought that because she came from a powerful family she escaped this fate. The font in Ruardean Church is of interest because it is one of a very few fonts to have been allowed into a church during the disturbances of the Civil War.

Ruardean was the birth place of Edward, James and Peter Horlick. At a young age James Horlick was taken by his parents to live in Cheltenham. He subsequently went to America and there perfected the formula for **Horlick's Malted Milk**. In 1895 James Horlick returned to Gloucestershire and bought Cowley Manor in the Cotswolds. He was responsible for the renovation of that building. He also paid for the village of Cowley to have a mains water supply.

With another son of Ruardean, Francis Brian, **James Horlick** returned to the village of his birth in 1905 and the two presented Ruardean with a **pair of bells** to make an octave of eight in the church tower. Francis Brian and James Horlick were both subsequently knighted.

Ruardean has a tradition of having a mayor of their ancient village.

Returning to the Nailbridge crossroads, turn left on to the A4136. From the crossroads can be seen a church built on gently rising land on the left of the road. This is the **Holy Trinity church** of **Drybrook**. There were no churches within the forest proper until the early years of the nineteenth century. This church was built in 1817 by the Reverend Henry Berkin. It was widely thought that this was the first church to be built within the forest so it was given the name of The Forest Church. This was not true because the church at Christchurch, on the other side of the forest, had been built the year before. In the churchyard, just beyond the gate which leads from the roadway is a grave. The simple headstone says

JOHN HAYWARD
DEPARTED THIS LIFE-
18th. APRIL 1818-
AGED 21.

This is the grave of the last man from the Forest of Dean to be hanged for sheep stealing.

After the death of Henry Berkin in 1847 the living was taken over by the Reverend **Henry George Nicholls** M.A. The son of a baronet, he was a man of some distinction and a lot of zeal and did much progressive work in the parish. He never married. The Reverend H.G. Nicholls was incumbent at Drybrook from 1847 until 1866. In that time he gave to posterity the first record of life in the Forest - its people, its customs, its history and industries.

His books included the now famous and much sought after **Nicholl's Forest of Dean**. There was a reprint of this book in 1966 but it is still quite a rarity. H.G. Nicholls also wrote 'The Personalities of the Forest', and 'Iron making in the Olden Times'.

In 1866 the Reverend Nicholls left Drybrook because of ill-health. He died in London in 1867 at the age of 44.

The village of **Drybrook** is some distance from the church. The settlement grew up mostly in the middle years of the nineteenth century around the Dry Brook. Renowned for its musical excellence, Drybrook has a **Male Voice Choir**, a **Ladies Choir** and **Silver Band**. This is a legacy from the mining era when every village made its own music.

Just outside Drybrook on the **Ross Road** is a most unusual house. It was built in the nineteenth century by a local mine-owner. At one end it has a tower. This was built so that the owner could ascend and look over the woodlands to his mine out in the Forest and be sure that the men had got the smoke rising at the proper time. Because this house is built on the crest of a considerable hilltop it was given the name **Euroclydon** - after the wind which wrecked St. Paul's boat on the island of Malta.

On the A4136 from **Drybrook Church** the road climbs a steep hill from the descent, on the other side, there are impressive views over the valley of the River Severn. The next village is **Mitcheldean**. This is now dominated by the **Rank Xerox factory** complex. This industry has made Mitcheldean a place of some importance. In the years 1970-80 there was a workforce at Rank Xerox, Mitcheldean of between 4,000 to 5,000 people. When the mines closed in the Forest of Dean this factory at Mitcheldean was to be the major employer in the Forest. Mitcheldean provided the cradle for the nurturing and developing of the technically advanced process of xerography.

This ancient township has seen many changes. Once its importance was the fact that it was the last place people came to before entering the forest or the first place they came to after leaving Coleford to journey through the forest, which was full of perils for unwary travellers. There were no less than five inns in Mitcheldean at one time. There was also a judges lodgings. Here the circuit judge would rest on his way to or from Wales.

Judge Jeffreys stayed here on occasions.

Being just outside the forest, Mitcheldean was something of a commercial centre for the people on that side of the Forest. Like Ruardean, Mitcheldean was inclined towards feudalism with the Colchester-Weymss family who, even though they lived on Westbury-on-Severn, held extensive interests in Mitcheldean and district.

In 1710 the **Colchester-Weymss** built for themselves a rather splendid house on the hilltop overlooking the township of Mitcheldean. A great deal of money was spent on this and the grounds were quite extensive. A splendid **beechwalk** was laid out in the vicinity which is still a favourite walk for many people. This house was given the strange name of **The Wilderness**. It now belongs to the Gloucestershire County Council and is used as a field centre. The surrounding area has an abundance of things interesting to ornithologists, naturalists and geologists.

At the same time that the Wilderness House was built the Colchester-Weymss built a **market house** for the people of Mitcheldean. This market house has had many uses over the years. It eventually belonged to Rank Xerox who very generously gave the building to the Mitcheldean parish council who now use it as their meeting place and administrative centre.

Mitcheldean could have been an outpost for the Romans. Certainly many traces of Roman roads have been found in and around the place. Some of this ancient roadway is now lost beneath the present primary school building. It could also be seen behind a shop in the very centre of the village. This would indicate that it went from there under the site of the church.

Mitcheldean has a large church. Dedicated to **St. Michael** it stands in the heart of the village. Dating from the thirteenth century, traces of the original building can be found in the Lady Chapel, at the bottom of the tower and the entrance porch. The church was much enlarged in 1450. Over the place where the Rood Screen once was, are the **doom paintings**. These date from the fifteenth century.

The Colchester-Weymss' extensive holdings, which stretched into the border county of Herefordshire, were all sold after the First World War. The only tangible reminder of their powerful influence in the village of Mitcheldean are the quaint almshouses built in the middle years of the nineteenth century.

Mitcheldean still has evidence of past industries such as lime kilns and stone quarrying all around.

The A4136 travels on from Mitcheldean towards Gloucester. A short distance along the road, in a little valley beside a babbling brook, is the ancient **Hart's Barn Farm**. This red building has ancient origins. First mentioned in 1080, this house was where 'three couples of hounds were kept for the King's pleasure'. When the monarch or noblemen hunted in the forest it was to Hart's Barn Farm that they might come to rest and partake of refreshment from the well stocked pantry and cellar. For seven hundred years the house belonged to the **Sergeant's of Longhope**. They all now lie buried in the graveyard at Mitcheldean.

From Mitcheldean, cross straight over and follow the road marked Flaxley & Westbury on Severn. This is an unclassified road. At the top of the hill on the right is the local comprehensive school which has taken the ancient name of Mitcheldean - **Dene Magna**. Just beyond the school on a bend in the road there is a turning to the left. This area is known as Abenhall or, as it was called until more recent years, Abinghall.

Now a very small place, **Abenhall** was once equal in importance to Mitcheldean, lying as it does on the edge of the forest. Abenhall is looked down upon by **Plump**

Hill which stands 800 feet above sea level and carries the A4136 on its journey from Gloucester to Coleford. On a side road leading from the bend can be found a lovely old church which, like the one at Mitcheldean, is dedicated to **St. Michael.** It is, perhaps, the only church in this area to still have a mounting block just outside the main gate.

Few churches can be better situated than Abenhall Church, for it is surrounded by rich agricultural lands with a backdrop of the forest sweeping down to the deep valley below. This small church has one notable distinction: it is the church of the Freeminers of the Forest of Dean. Here the Freeminers hold any services they need to have. The font in the church is a treasured possession for it bears, on the eight panels of its octagonal shape, six with the coats of arms of important local families, including the Sergeants who once lived at Harts Barn Farm. The other two sides have the arms of the freeminers, six picks and two shovels, and the arms of the Free Smiths which are horseshoe tongs. The Freeminers arms can also be found on the stair turret.

This is a very interesting area. There are several traces of the Roman road which once traversed the Forest on its way to **Ariconium.** Returning to the main road and continuing in the direction of **Flaxley** on the left can be found the ruins of an iron foundry at **Guns Mills house.** Once cannon were made at this place giving the house its name. More recently it was a paper mill. Now it is a private residence.

Behind Guns Mills, beneath a steep wooded hillside which has a Jacob's ladder to make climbing it possible, is **St. Anthony's well.** This is perhaps the best watercourse in the Dean, certainly it is the most beautiful, lying as it does in the woodlands. This well supplied the water to the abbey farther down the valley. It was dedicated to St. Anthony, the patron saint of hogs, by the monks from the abbey. The waters of the well keep a constant temperature of fifty degrees in winter and summer. It was claimed that the waters from the well had healing properties and many people came to test these claims. It was supposed to cure rheumatics if the sufferer went to the well on the first day of May and descended the first step down to the water, then on the consecutive days returned and went a step lower each day until on the ninth day the person seeking the cure would be on the bottom and completely submerged in the ice cold water. If no cure was affected by this drastic attempt then the sufferer had to wait another year before trying the cure again.

The waters were also said to be good for troubles of the eyes, skin complaints, and a cure for mangy dogs. There is no doubt that the waters of the well did contain some mineral properties which had been of benefit to certain people at times.

Beyond Guns Mills on the Flaxley road can be seen a much renovated Mill House known as **Flaxley Mill.** It was the last working mill in the Forest and finished as such in 1912.

This area was the home of **Kitty Drew** the nineteenth century self taught poetess. She was just an ordinary working girl who had a strange feel for words and wrote some powerful verse which is still much quoted today. This poem, written in 1835, is probably one of the best remembered of her works:-

'In days of old 'twas here and there a cot,
Of architecture they'd little knowledge got;
None but a few free miners then lived here,
Who thought no harm to catch a good fat deer,
Or steal an oak - it was their chief delight
Old foresters I'm told, did think t'was right.....'

This is the start of the lovely vale of Castiard, or the valley of the chestnuts. The waters from St. Anthony's well flow through this valley and makes it a lush and verdant area. Several cottages of some age and character stand beside the stream making a picture of rural bliss. Amongst the woodlands which sweep down to the road side which winds through this valley can be found, in the early springtime, wild garlic and bluebells which vie with the wood anemone, the windflower, and the star of Bethlehem for pride of place amongst the tall trees. It is a valley of peace and quiet.

The road meanders between woodlands and green fields to where, at the end of the valley, stands the glory that is **Flaxley Abbey.** It was the only abbey ever to have been built within the forest.

In the year 1143 when the Forest of Dean belonged to **Milo Fitzwalter**, Earl of Hereford, who lived in the castle at Gloucester, on Christmas Eve he galloped over the Westgate bridge which spanned the river Severn to hunt in his Forest of Dean.

When the party were deep in the forest, somehow Milo got separated from the rest of the company. When he was quite alone he was shot and fatally wounded by an unseen bowman. His killer was never found. On the spot where Milo Fitzwalter was mortally wounded his son, Roger, caused a Cistercian abbey to be built. It was dedicated to **St. Mary de Dene.**

The monks lived very comfortably in the abbey in the beautiful valley. Important travellers making their way to the Forest of Dean would stay at Gloucester Castle then journey to the abbey, rest there, then journey on to St. Briavel's Castle.

Flaxley Abbey

The monks had their iron forges in the vale of Castiard, and King Henry III gave them **Abbot's Wood** nearby to produce the timber with which to fire their forges.

The Abbey at Flaxley was suppressed in 1536 when a survey of income was taken. Flaxley needed £200 in annual income to survive, but their income in the crucial year was only £112.12.1p so the monks were turned out of their abbey. The king gave Flaxley to a particular favourite of his, **Sir William Kingston**, the Constable of the Tower of London. With the abbey went extensive possessions around the area. The Kingstons, father and son, did much to destroy essential parts of the original abbey.

The abbey was purchased, by the **Boevey Family,** who owned it for 313 years. Iron forges worked in the Flaxley valley until the early years of the nineteenth century.

The Flaxley Abbey was bought in 1960 by **the late Mr. Baden Watkins.** He and his wife did a great deal to restore the abbey and renovated much of the fabric of the place. He also wrote a well researched history of the abbey which is still available locally. The abbey is not open to the public. Mr. Watkins allowed the house and grounds to be used for village events. Following his death in 1994, the house remains in his family.

High above Flaxley is **Welshbury Hill**. This was a hill-fort and many implements of the Neolithic and Mesolithic age have been discovered here. It is one of the most interesting archaeological sites in the forest area. The hill is a high prominence, a feature which would have made it a desirable site for a fortress, commanding views over the surrounding countryside which would have been an essential part of a defence.

Two roads lead out of Flaxley. The one leading to the left goes to **Blaisdon**. This is a country road which passes through high hedged agricultural land. On this road can be glimpsed, on the left, the splendour of Blaisdon Hall built amongst considerable surrounding land which belongs to the estate.

The village has houses which bear names such as The Old Forge and Mill Cottage. Blaisdon has won awards for being so beautifully kept. It is hard to realise that in 1699 a fire broke out in the village smithy which destroyed nearly all the village in a very short time.

A church has stood on the site of the present **St. Michael's Church** since the thirteenth century. Extensive renovations were done during 1867 and the cost borne by the man who was, at that time. owner of the Blaisdon estates.

Blaisdon Hall, which is approached under an impressive archway, was built at great cost by **Edwin Crawshay**, the son of the man who paid for the renovation of the church. The Crawshays were at that time wealthy owners of iron and coal interests in the Forest of Dean. The estates became the possessions of the Stubbs family who were from Warrington. **Peter Stubbs** brought fame to the place with his famous shire horse **Blaisdon Conquerer**, the bones of which are still in the Natural History Museum.

Since 1935 the Blaisdon Hall and estates have been owned by the Salesians of the Roman Catholic church. They have kept the house and estates in superb order.

Perhaps Blaisdon's greatest claim to fame is the **Blaisdon red plum**. This small place has given its name to one of the best cooking and eating plums in this country. The plum was first grown at the **Tanhouse Farm**, in the late years of the nineteenth century, by John Dowding.

From Blaisdon a road leads on to the A4136 Gloucester highway.

The other route which could have been taken out of Flaxley leads a short distance past the unused Flaxley School. Here is signposted **Pope's Hill**. This hill is well worth ascending, and in order to see the superb views which are commanded from its height there are good r oads.

When Catharina Boevey lived at the abbey in the late seventeenth to early eighteenth century, she had a friend come to stay for a month. The lady actually stayed for almost forty years. Each morning, this friend, whose name was **Joan Pope**, would take a walk up the hill opposite the Abbey. The hill took her name and has, since that time, been known as **Pope's Hill**.

The road from the diversion to below Pope's Hill leads to the A48 Chepstow to Gloucester road. In the direction of Gloucester is the Severnside town of Westbury.

Most of the towns and villages which stand beside the River Severn on the A48 side, have individual charm. **Westbury-on-Severn** is attractive even to those who merely pass through on the busy road. The Church of **St. Peter, St. Paul and St. Mary** is unusual in that the tower is separate from the church. The tower is one of a few detached church towers in Gloucestershire and stands about fifty feet from the church building. It was built in 1270 as a stronghold and a place to which the people of the village could withdraw in times of trouble. Situated so close to Wales, the men of Westbury often had to cope with incursions into their territory. There are arrow slits in the tower and other indications of its original purpose.

The large church also dates from the thirteenth century. It was the centre of some activity in the Civil War. During the siege of Gloucester, in 1643, there was a small garrison of Parliamentary troops in Westbury. They defected to the Royalist cause. After the siege was broken, Colonel Massey marched to Westbury, where the garrison was holding the church and nearby **Westbury Court**, and defeated them.

The houses facing the church are always a pleasing sight in the months of summer with their pretty gardens and hanging baskets.

There is a walk from Westbury which goes to the river. This leads to a part of the river where commercial shipping on the river is still carried on. From here also, the **Garden Cliffs** can be seen. These cliffs rise from the river and have yielded many interesting fossils. The river is not to be trusted. It is famous for the **Bore tide** which is particularly spectacular in the springtime and early autumn. The tide whispers up the river so quietly and quickly that it can be very dangerous.

Once Westbury-on-Severn was the home of the very rich and powerful family of Colchester Weymss. They owned **Westbury Court** for many hundreds of years until the house was demolished in the middle years of the twentieth century. All that now remains of the house, and the vast estates which this family once owned, are the **Dutch water gardens** which are now administered by the National Trust. They are open to the public.

Although the main **South Wales railway** runs in close proximity to the village of Westbury-on-Severn there are no facilities for boarding trains in this locality.

From Westbury it is not far to the ancient township of **Newnham** which is built on gently rising land alongside the river. The drive along the A48 in the direction of Newnham is pleasant and passes through Broadoak.

The White Hart Inn at Broadoak dates back to about 1780. **Broadoak** once depended on the river to provide much of the employment for those who lived there. Now it has to be protected from the flow of the river with flood barriers. It is an excellent spot from which to watch the Bore tide.

Newnham-on-Severn is one of the most pleasant of the riverside settlements. There was a ford across the river here. Some people believe that this is where the Romans made their first crossing of the Severn to make their early forays into the Forest of Dean.

There was a ferry service here since the early thirteenth century. This linked the town of Newnham, on the right bank, with **Arlingham** on the other side. Many men of royal birth knew Newnham. **King John**, that inveterate traveller, presented a great sword to the borough of Newnham. It has a blade more than four feet long and at six feet in total is one of the longest swords in England. It has an inscription showing that it was repaired at a later date. Also at Newnham in 1171 the Earl of Pembroke met **Henry II** who, with his army, was just preparing to depart to Ireland.

Newnham also once had a castle which stood at the place where **Castle House** now stands on the green.

Newnham became an important place in the nineteenth century because in 1851 a railway was opened there. This meant that people were able to move much farther afield in greater comfort with considerably more speed. The large houses which grace the old township bear witness to its one time importance. Down some of the streets, such as **Passage Way**, can be seen brief glimpses of the river.

Because of its importance as a riverside town, Newnham also had a good number of Inns. **The Victoria**, once a private residence, dates from the eighteenth century and used to have, set in the window on the staircase, a piece of old glass illustrating the fable of the ant and the grasshopper. This was stolen.

The Church of **St. Peter**, Newnham's parish church stands at the top of the **High Street** opposite the Victoria Hotel. It stands on the **Nab**, an area of high land which protrudes towards the Severn and is washed at the base by the waters of the river.

This is not Newnham's first church. The original church was in danger of being washed away by the river so a new site was found and this church was built in 1366. It is thought that Riverdale, now **Brightlands School** stands near, or on, the site of the original church. Newnham is built immediately on the famous horseshoe bend in the river.

Most of the villages and townships on the edge of the Forest had pounds and facilities for impounding the sheep or any other animal which strayed from the free grazing areas of the Forest. These would be released only on the payment of a fine by the owners. Although instances of **'Pound Cottages'** can still be found around the peripheral area of the Forest all the high walled square pounds seem to have disappeared. Only Newnham seems to have preserved its Pound intact. Of course it is not now used for its original purpose.

Mrs Annie Wood, who wrote *'King's Lynne'*, lived at **Newnham House** and it is said she depicted the house in her writings. The story of Newnham has been told in an excellent book written by Mabel K. Woods.

The A48 descends from Newnham down a short cliff lined road. On the left the river can clearly be seen. **Bullo Pill** is the next place of interest along this road. It is a short distance from the main highway tucked away just beyond the railway bridge. Once this sleepy little

place bustled with activity for, from here, coal from the Forest pits was shipped out to places in the Midlands and south-west of England. At the little pill it is still possible to see traces of the chute which was used to load the coal trows. The coal was brought down from the Forest by various means, latterly by rail.

All along this stretch of the river can be found traces of the days when coal shipping was an all important activity here. Many of the people who live in this tiny place have memories of, or connections with, shipping on the Severn.

Travelling along the A48 towards Lydney, on the right a splendid Mansion House can be seen. This is **Oaklands Park** which now belongs to the **Camphill Trust**. This house was built in the revived Palladian style in 1840 by Henry Crawshay, the man who had so many industrial interests in the Forest of Dean. He came from a wealthy family of ironmasters in Merthyr Tydfil. When he came to the Forest of Dean he was already wealthy and he built a considerable industrial empire in the Dean.

It is said that it was Henry Crawshay who built Cinderford to house the people who were brought into the forest to work in the ironworks and in his iron and coal mines. For the 130 years that the

Lightmoor colliery worked, in the woods near Cinderford, it was owned by the Crawshay company. They also owned many of the other important Forest mines. Henry Crawshay was a generous benefactor. He paid for the expensive renovation of Newnham Church, Awre Church and Blaisdon Church. His eldest son, Edwin, built Blaisdon Hall. It was from this mansion house that the four poster beds and other furniture were acquired by the Speech House.

Immediately opposite the entrance to Oaklands Park is a turning to **Awre**. This is an ancient riverside settlement. The area is agricultural and is reached by travelling down a country road for about two miles.

Awre is on the opposite side of the River Severn to the **Wildfowl Trust at Slimbridge** and although once the river was very much closer to Awre, it has over the years moved away to the Slimbridge side.

In the River Severn, between Awre and Slimbridge, is the great sandbank known as the **Noose** and close by, stretching farther down the river towards Lydney, are the **Frampton sands.** Both of these stretches of golden sands are exposed at low tides and it is probably from them that Awre got its name. It is a derivation of Aurum meaning gold.

Awre is a quiet place. In the area are several ancient farmhouses but the thing for which this riverside place is now noted is the salmon which are caught here. The village is dominated by the grey edifice of the old church of **St. Andrews** which stands in its midst.

Awre is such a removed place that it could seem as if the world has passed it by. However, it has put its mark on every church and cathedral in the land. For by the riverside at Awre was born **John Hopkins**. With Thomas Sternhold, from nearby Blakeney, they set the psalms to metrical verse. It was in the church at Awre that the Psalms of David were first sung to music. It is claimed that the Psalms, so set, were to be the third best selling book in the world, after the Bible and the book of Common Prayer.

There is in the church a chest claimed to be one thousand years old. This was made, and roughly hollowed, from the trunk of a tree. It is locally known as the mortuary for it was once used as a repository for dead bodies recovered from the river. Today it is used for much more mundane purposes.

Close to Awre are two farms, **Box** and **Little Box**. It is thought that these two places could have been used as hunting lodges by King John.

Some distance down the river from Awre is the tiny place known as **Gatcombe**. Here there stands a house of some age. This is where **Drake**, the famous admiral, used to stay when he came down to the area to select timbers for his ships from the oaks of the nearby Forest of Dean.

The small creek in front of the house still fills with river water when the great tides surge up the Severn. Now, however, this fascinating house is separated from the river by the main South Wales railway line.

Gatcombe was not always such a quiet place. In the early years of the nineteenth century much of the business of shipping out Forest of Dean coal was lost to Newnham and transferred to Gatcombe.

On the A48 **Blakeney** is the next place of importance beyond Newnham. It is a village of some size, with some quite large houses, stretching beside this main road. This is the village of **Thomas Sternhold** and his house still stands in Blakeney. He died in 1549.

Blakeney Church stands at the bottom of the steep road which leads into the village. It was only built late in the nineteenth century although there was a great religious surge in the area long before that time.

Behind the village of Blakeney is the Forest of Dean and it starts at a place called **Brains Green**. The name of Brain is a very common one in the Forest. It is said that many hundreds of years ago a family of that name were leaving Ireland by sea to go to some other country. A great storm arose after they had been at sea some while. The ship was at the mercy of the elements and was blown to safety up the Severn to Lydney. Here the family thankfully went ashore and decided this was as good as place as any to settle. There have been many variations on the name such as Brayne, Braine and of course Brain. The family of that name flourished and multiplied. Now they have scattered to all parts of the world and have made their mark in many fields of life. There are still a large number people who bear that name in the forest.

From the roadway which passes through Brains Green can be seen two semi detached house one of which has gravestones in the garden. Early in the nineteenth century, Dissenters from the established church were beginning to be very active in this place. In 1823, a Tabernacle one mile north of Blakeney was built with a graveyard. This Tabernacle was replaced by another, which was built in Blakeney in 1849, before an established church was built there. The original Tabernacle built in 1825 became the two house we now see. The last burial took place in the graveyard in 1930 when a son of William Morgan, one of the founders of the original Tabernacle, was buried there with his father.

Situated on the edge of the Forest, **Viney Hill** looks down upon Blakeney and the A48. It is so called because once vines grew upon its hilly sides. The church, built in 1866, also serves Yorkley. It has a distinctive round tower.

From Blakeney the A48 leads to Lydney.

LYDNEY
Gloucester - 20 miles
Chepstow - 9 miles
Newport - 26 miles
Cheltenham - 27
Tourist Information -
  Hams RoadTel.
  (0594)844894
Harbour Authority -
  Severn Trent, Pier Head
Library - Hill Street

See Gazetteer for leisure and recreational facilities

There has been a settlement in the area of **Lydney** even before Roman times.

Lydney's importance has come from its position on the navigable River Severn. Lydney has had a **harbour** for many hundreds of years and today there is still a yachting club here.

Today Lydney is a very busy place with traffic passing through on the A48. This problem will end when the by-pass around the place is completed.

A thriving town, Lydney has its share of business and social activities, and it has a long and extremely interesting history.

Lydney also has some splendid areas for recreation such as **Bathurst Park**, a public park presented to Lydney by **Charles Bathurst** of **Lydney Park** and named after him. Also the **Lydney Recreation Ground**. These two places provide facilities for boating, model boat sailing, bowls, tennis, football, miniature golf and putting, cricket and rugby.

In the area of Lydney has been found evidence of settlement in the Bronze age. There have been many indications of a pre-historic community. The Romans, of course, left much tangible evidence of their time in Lydney for this was a place on the route used by the Romans from Gloucester to South Wales.

The river has played a very important part in the life of Lydney. From the docks here sailed out **William Wintour** who was a vice admiral. He went to meet the might of the Spanish Armada who, it is claimed, were under instructions to destroy the Forest of Dean. In the forest was grown sesile oak which provided the timber, said to be stronger than iron, from which the ships defending England were made.

The Armada was defeated and William Wintour was rewarded with land on which he built **Whitecross House**. His grandson inherited the house and destroyed it at the time of the Civil War. Today, near the site of that house, stands **Whitecross School**.

Lydney Cross and High Street

In the seventeenth century **ship-building** was being carried out at Lydney. It was an extremely busy port. In the nineteenth, and into the twentieth century, Lydney was the most important dock for the transporting of forest coal by water. **Coal ships** were an accepted and very usual sight in the Lydney docks and for some

time the chutes for loading remained at the waterside.

Near the harbour stands the sixteenth century **Naas House**. This is an impressive building with a tower and distinctive cupola.

St. Mary's Church dates from before the thirteenth century. Some remains of the earliest part of the church can be found in the lower part of the tower, which has lancet windows, and several moulded, early English arches. St. Mary's stands on the site of what was possibly a much older church.

The Lydney Cross is a very ancient and interesting feature of the town. It stands in a prominent position at the top of **Church Street**. This cross was thoroughly restored in 1878 by the family of the **Reverend W.H. Bathurst** of Lydney Park as a memorial to that gentleman. A marble tablet at the base of the cross is inscribed to this effect. It was once used as a preaching cross.

Close to the Cross is **Lydney Town Hall**. The foundation stone for this building was laid in 1888 by **Charles Bathurst**. The building was completed one year later.

Lydney has a railway station on its outskirts on the Gloucester-South Wales line. The railways are remembered here. On the site of the one time Norchard colliery there is the **Norchard Steam Preservation Society.** This is to be found on the B4234 Forest Road leading to Parkend. Here are preserved tangible memories of the splendid days of the steam railways. A length of track has been re-laid and working engines take visitors to the town centre on trips along the length of the present track in the railway carriages of another era. There is an excellent museum of railway memorabilia which can also be visited. The centre is run by volunteers who are all railway enthusiasts.

Once the **Severn Bridge**, which carried the railway across the river, was near Lydney. It was a wonderful engineering feat. Built in 1879, trains passed over its length until it was partly destroyed, in 1960, when it was hit by a tanker. This was one of the worst disasters ever to take place on the waters of the River Severn. Later, as a result of this accident, the bridge was demolished.

Motorised public transport came early to Lydney and the surrounding area, largely through the efforts and the tenacity of **John Hylton Watts**. He was an undoubted pioneer in the field of public transport. As early as 1921, Mr. Watts began to operate a service with three buses in the densely populated areas of South Wales. He called this venture The Valleys Motor Bus Service. It was an extremely popular innovation. After the success of his first venture, Mr. Watts turned his attentions to the needs on his own doorstep. He formed the Lydney and Dean Forest Bus Services. This service provided public transport for Lydney people to Coleford, and through the forest to Gloucester, **The Red and White Bus Services** were formed by an amalgamation of companies in 1934, and Mr. Watts was to be Chairman.

Mr. John Watts' public transport interests became international. He was a man who had achieved greatness in his chosen field through his own endeavours. He had a great affection for his town of Lydney and was a most generous benefactor. He gave the **Lydney British Legion** their own premises and a bungalow for the steward. The recreation ground, which is such a wonderful asset to Lydney, was made possible through John Watts. He was the driving force behind the project and, with Viscount Bledisloe, gave the land for the Recreation Trust.

A keen follower of Lydney sporting activities Mr. Watts helped in every possible way to promote so many things which brought richness and interest to the lives of the people of Lydney.

On Mr. Watts 75th birthday he was honoured by his town of Lydney with a luncheon in the town hall. The biggest carnival Lydney has ever had was staged, and a parade 'Transport of the Century' was featured. Mr. Watts was presented with a illuminated address in recognition of his most generous support of Lydney's many activities and projects.

The Watts company still flourishes in Lydney today and provides employment for a large number of people.

Lydney Park House is situated on a commanding hilltop in extensive grounds just outside the town of Lydney and can be seen from the A48. The manor of Lydney, which had belonged to the **Wintour** or Winter family, passed to the **Bathurst family** in 1723.

The Bathursts had a mansion house built lower down the hill from the site of the present house. Then, in 1875, it was replaced by the present building which stands at the top of the hill where the family still live. The Bathurst family have been very much part of the life of the town of Lydney. They have participated in many aspects of the life of the place. This interest included the building of **Lydney Hospital**. In 1882 Mrs. Elizabeth Bathurst decided that a hospital was needed for the sick of the district.

The first hospital was opened at Aylburton in 1882. It was known as the **Lydney and Aylburton Cottage Hospital**. The present Lydney Hospital now stands on land on the Bream road donated by Viscount Bledisloe in 1907.

Mr. Melville Watts, nephew of John Watts, who in his lifetime did much for Lydney Hospital generally, is now the dedicated and hardworking chairman of the Friends of Lydney Hospital. He was made an M.B.E. in 1993. He is also a Verderer of the Forest of Dean.

The grounds of the Bathurst home, **Lydney Park**, contains some of the best Roman remains in the country. These are on a hilltop in the estate and include a hospitium, a bath house and the celebrated temple to the British god Nodens. Much interest was aroused by the artefacts discovered amongst the remains of the Roman occupation. They include the famous **Lydney Dog** which is now in the British Museum in London as well as coins, pottery, ornaments, various implements and even a metal plaque showing Nodens himself as a young god in a chariot drawn by four prancing horses. He was accompanied by winged figures who represented the winds. The eminent archaeologist, **Sir Mortimer Wheeler,** came to Lydney to make a detailed investigation of the site.

The town of Lydney has a famous son. **Dr. Herbert Howells** the music composer was born here in 1892. He was educated in Lydney. He became a close friend of **F.W. Harvey** the poet. Herbert Howells studied organ music under Herbert Brewer at Gloucester Cathedral with **Ivor Gurney**, another Gloucestershire poet. For some years Dr. Herbert Howells was Professor of Music at London University. He wrote music services for all the major cathedrals in this country and specialised in choral music. One of his major works was a Requiem to his son Michael.

The daughter of Herbert Howells is the star of the stage and television, Ursula Howells.

The most eminent of Lydney's sons was **Viscount Bledisloe** (1867 -1958.) He was a barrister and a Member of Parliament for the South Wilton Division of Wiltshire in 1910. He was a Parliamentary Secretary, Privy Councillor, Knight of the British Empire and Knight Grand Cross of the Most Distinguished Order of St. Michael. From 1930 to 1935 he was Governor General of New Zealand. In 1935 he became the Viscount Bledisloe, 1st Baron of Lydney and Aylburton. Viscount Bledisloe was also the senior Verderer of the Forest of Dean.

The next village, a mile of so along the A48, is the village of Aylburton.

There is a tendency to hurry through **Aylburton** for the village suffers much from speeding traffic. The houses and shops in this place cling to the sides of the main road and every attempt to cross, from one side to the other, is something of an achievement. Even though the practice is to pass through as quickly as possible it is well worth pausing to take a closer look.

There is in the village one of the finest **preaching crosses** in the whole locality. It is fourteenth century and stands about sixteen feet high. It is decorated with four niches. This cross once stood in the centre of the main street. Because of the great increase in traffic flow it has now been moved to the side of the road.

Aylburton is quite near to the River Severn, separated by the railway which passes close to the river. This means that the village does have fishing interests, for Severn salmon are a much sought fish. Shrimps are another local harvest from the river. Agriculture is also a feature of life here and the river side meadows are good pasture land.

The Lydney Park estate is a little closer to Aylburton than it is to Lydney. In consequence the help and generosity of the Bledisloe family has been very much a part of life here. People from Aylburton are employed on the Lydney Park estate.

The **primary school** in Aylburton owes its existence to the Bathurst family. The site on which the school stands was given by the Reverend W.H. Bathurst who also contributed generously towards the actual building.

Until 1857 **St Mary's**, the parish church of Aylburton, was standing on a hill overlooking the village. In that year the church was removed from its elevated position and brought, stone by stone, down to its present site at the bottom of the hill just on the edge of the village. With the church came the fifteenth century stone pulpit. This is quite a rarity for there are only about sixty of these stone pulpits in existence in this country. The cost of rebuilding the church on its new site was paid for by Charles Bathurst with the exception of £25 which was given by the lessees of the great tithes. A small plaque on the side of the church records these events.

On the hilly land behind Aylburton is the **Common** where the people who live there area community in their own right, quite separate from the village of Aylburton.

Dr. C. Scott Garrett, who was for some time the President of the

Forest of Dean Local History Society, lived at **Sandford House** on Aylburton Common. One day, when a hole was being dug for a post to be put in, some Roman pottery was found. Dr. Scott Garrett investigated and oversaw excavations at the spot and several extensive Roman buildings were unearthed. It was thought they could have been storehouses.

The A48 leads from Aylburton to another village which also spreads both sides of this road. It is Alvington which is linked, in particular ecclesiastically, with its neighbour farther up the A48 **Woolaston**.

Both these villages are in close proximity to the river and both have strong farming connections. The two places are separated not only by a stretch of roadway but also the Cone valley. This is a water course which is fed from springs which rise on the high ground behind Woolaston and Alvington.

Geographically this area is the narrowing peninsula between Severn and Wye. Consequently the areas of Tintern, Lancaut, Chepstow and Tidenham are closely linked with the life and history of the settlements along this stretch of the A48.

Alvington is very much a community in its own right and

today is a place concerned with conservation.

The village of **Woolaston** is, to the right of the A48, spreading out beneath the heights behind. One of the most impressive things about both Alvington and Woolaston are the views from the hills which rise to St. Briavels, Hewelsfield and Tidenham Chase. From here it is possible to look away across the Severn valley and as expressed by a Woolaston resident, 'It feels as if you are looking at things from an aeroplane'. The views one gets are quite spectacular at all times of the year but particularly so when nature has touched the countryside with the colours of the autumn.

The Cone valley, which is now very nearly the accepted boundary between the parishes of Alvington and Woolaston, was once the boundary between England and Wales, or so local legend claims.

Some of the water which feeds the Cone brook comes from **St. Annes Well** which is just under the hillside of St. Briavels. Industry was once concentrated around the waters of this brook. At its source was the **Rodmore Mill**. This was where the farmers from the surrounding farms would take their grain for milling. Below the Rodmore Mill the waters of the brook were dammed and diverted to form the **Clanna**

Lakes. This beautiful area which has a mansion house was, with much of Alvington, Woolaston, Sedbury, some of Tidenham and Hewelsfield, in the possession of the **Marling family** of **Sedbury Park** for some years.

Following the death of Col. Sir Percival Scrope Marling in 1919 the estates were sold in 1921 and there were dramatic changes. Previously much of the land and the farms in the area had belonged to the Beaufort estates.

There were other mills on the brook which utilised the water for industrial purposes. Finally the brook empties into Cone Pill beside the Severn.

Woolaston Manor was granted to the Monks by Richard de Clare, the founder of Tintern Abbey, in 1131 at the same time the abbey was built. It was to be, for the monks, their greatest asset until 1535 when, in the reign of Henry VIII, the abbey was dissolved and the roof lifted.

At **Woolaston Grange** there was a medieval chapel, built by the monks of Tintern. The chapel gradually deteriorated over the years. It was used as a farm building for some time but now it is no more.

Burnt House at **Brookend** is said to have got its name because the residents in this house failed to rally to the cause of the Roundheads during the Civil War and so had their house burnt around them. Obviously it was rebuilt. The name of **Possession House**, which dates from the seventeenth century, also gives cause for speculation.

Alvington's **Village Hall** was built on land, given to the village for that purpose, by **Mr. W.A. Thomas** who was the publican at the **Blacksmith's Arms** for many years. He loved his village and gave generously to improve life for the community there.

The **Village Hall** in Woolaston was built through the efforts of the people of the place who were encouraged by the late Mr. John Watts who made a generous donation, over a period of years, on the understanding that a legal trust deed was established as a War Memorial.

It is obvious that for many years there has been activity on the river here at Woolaston, and in the locality. **The Cone Pill** makes a splendid small harbour, not used now because of the silting and the fact that there is now not the demand for river borne transport. It was used in Roman times and, in a field significantly called Chesters to the east of Woolaston Grange, a **Roman villa** has been unearthed. There was thought to have been a small lighthouse at the Roman villa

to guide shipping safely into the small pills which were landing places.

Until the mills of the Cone valley were closed, paper was shipped out from the Pill, as was iron ore and other commodities.

Fishing was also an industry in this area, with Severn salmon the prize. There are records of fishing taking place here long before Tintern Abbey was built.

Access to the river is now some what restricted by the South Wales railway. When the railway opened in 1851, Woolaston had its own railway station. This station was at some distance from the village and was used mostly for the transporting of goods. It is now closed.

Stroat, the next village on the A48 as it travels towards Chepstow, is a small scattered settlement. It has one very interesting feature which is the **Broad Stone**. This standing stone can only be found by walking across the fields towards the river bank. There is a path from the side of the **Evangelical Church** in Stroat. The railway line now runs between the Broad Stone and the River Severn. It is thought that it once marked a passage across the River Severn at this point. It is also conjectured that once the Broad Stone was the start of a trackway which led up from the banks of the river to Tidenham Chase. Used at one time by pack-horses, this track led through the heights, between the two rivers, then down to Brockweir in the Wye Valley where there was a river crossing. The distance from Severn to Wye about four miles.

Certainly the Broad Stone did have some significance at one time. Today it is remembered in folklore. These tell of the legendary Jack o' Kent who carried on a lifelong feud with the devil, defeating the evil one in every contest particularly when it came to throwing stones across the wide waters of the River Severn.

The roadside boundary of **Stroat House** was moved nearer to the building some years ago when the A48 was widened. Fortunately the wall was rebuilt with the original materials. The present day house, which is surrounded by a high stone wall, has, over the years, been much improved and carefully renovated. It was originally a large stone farmhouse built in 1690 possibly on the site of an even older, smaller, house.

At one time the house was owned by a Captain Fenton who fought with Wellington during the wars of 1808-1812. Evidence of this family's residence at Stroat House can still be seen in the form of writing etched in the window pane of a first floor window. It

says -

"Fanny and Cary are two naughty girls for not being there to recieve their dear brother. Charles H. Fenton (Capt.) 53rd. Regiment."

Stroat House is a very fine residence. From the east side of the house the windows look accross fields to the wide water of the River Severn. The Broad Stone can also been seen quite clearly. Stroat House and **Stroat Farm** are two large houses for such a small hamlet as Stroat. Stroat has not expanded as did its neighbouring villages although it did once have its own pub The George and Dragon (now closed). Stroat is much affected by modern life in that the flow of traffic along the A48 tends to take away some of the charm of this place. It does have several buildings of interest, including Stroat House, which dates from the seventeenth century and the Stroat Farm.

From Stroat it is but a short distance to the ceaseless rush of traffic flowing over the Severn Bridge, and the town of Chepstow, where the demands of present day life integrate with the history of yesterday.

'Journey done, their ceaseless flow
Could neither pause nor tarry.
Beneath the shadow of the bridge
Sweet Wye and Severn marry.'

Tourist Information Offices

Coleford
27 Market St. Coleford
Tel: (0594) 836307
Mon-Sat 10am-5pm
Sun 10am-2pm
(Bank hols-Jul/Aug only)

Newent
Newent Library, High St
Tel: (0531) 822145
Mon/Thur/Sat 10am-5pm
Tue/Fri 10am-7pm
closed 1pm-2pm

Monmouth
Shire Hall,
Agincourt Sq.
Tel: (0600) 713899

Lydney
13 Hamms Rd, Lydney
Tel: (0594) 844894

Cinderford
12 Belleview Rd, Cinderford
Tel: (0594) 823184

Chepstow
The Gatehouse
High St. Tel: (0296) 23772

Ross On Wye
20 Broad St. Ross
Tel: (0989) 62768
Easter-Sept Mon-Sat 9.30-5.30pm
August (plus Sun) 10.00-4.00pm
Oct-Easter Mon-Sat 10.00-4.00pm

Symonds Yat
Wye Valley Visitor Centre, Symonds Yat West
Tel: (0600) 890360
March-Oct Mon-Sun 10.00-5.00pm
Oct-March (except Mon/Fri) 10.00-4.00pm

Public Toilets

Lydney - Library Car Park **Newent** - Lewall Street Car Park **Monmouth** - cattle market
Chepstow - St. Anne St + Bank St Car Park **Ross On Wye** - Brookend Street Car Park
The Crofts, Wye Street

The Shambles

A Museum of Victorian Life

Delightful Museum set out as a COMPLETE VICTORIAN TOWN of shops, cottages and houses, cobbled streets, gas lamps and alleyways, rural and town trades and crafts.

A staggeringly large collection in an unexpectedly spacious location near the centre of this attractive market town.

Church Street, Newent, Gloucestershire 0531 822144
Open: - Tuesday - Sunday and Bank Holiday Mondays
10.00am - 6.00pm
(last admission 5.00pm or dusk if earlier)
MID MARCH - END DECEMBER
RESTAURANT *(seasonal opening - licensed)* **GIFT SHOPS**

Beauty Spots & Viewpoints

Nagshead Nature Reserve - Parkend + Symonds Yat, **Kymin, Yat Rock, Devil's Pulpit,**
Wintours Leap

Picnic Sites

Beechenhurst off B4226; **Wenchford** B4431; **New Fancy View** 1 mile south of Speech House;
Symonds Yat Rock west of B4228; **Edge End** A4136; **Mallards Pike** B4431;
Speech House Woodland B4226; Blaize Bailey between Littledean and Soudley.

Early Closing & Market Days

AREA	EARLY CLOSING	MARKET	CATTLE MARKET
Coleford	Thursday	Thursday	
Lydney	Thursday	Saturday	
Cinderford	Thursday	Friday	
Newent	Wednesday	Friday	
Ross On Wye	Wednesday	Thursday	Friday
		Saturday	
Chepstow	Wednesday	Sunday (racecourse)	
Monmouth	Thursday	Friday	Monday
		Saturday	

Museums

The Shambles,
16-20 Church St., Newent
Tel: (0531) 822144

The Button Museum & Craft Shop,
Kyrie St. Ross On Wye
Tel: (0989) 66089

Wye Valley Heritage Centre
Doward, Whitchurch, Ross
Tel: (0600) 89047

Dean Heritage Centre
Soudley, Nr Cinderford
Tel: (0594) 822170

The Lost Street Museum
Palma Court, 27 Brookend St. Ross
Tel: (0989) 62752

The Castle Regiment Museum
Monmouth
Tel: (0600) 772175

Chepstow Museum
Bridge St. Chepstow
Tel: (0291) 625981

The Nelson Museum
Priory St. Monmouth
Tel: (0600) 713519

Sporting Facilities

GOLF: **St. Pierre Park Chepstow**
Gwent Tel: (0291) 625261

Rolls of Monmouth Golf Club
Monmouth . Tel: (0600)

CYCLING: **Pedalabikeaway Cycle Centre,**
Cannop Valley.
Tel: (0594) 860065
GENERAL: **Chepstow & District Leisure Centre,**
Crossway Green, Chepstow.
Tel: (0291) 623832

Littledean Trekking Centre,
Wellington Farm, Littledean.
Tel: (0594) 823955

The Royal Forest of Dean Golf Club
Lords Hill, Coleford
Tel: (0594) 832583
Lydney Golf Club, The Links,
Lydney. Tel: (0594) 842614

Wyedean Canoe & Adventure Centre,
Hollybarn, Symonds Yat.
Tel: (0594) 833238

Dean Heritage Centre

The best place to start your visit to Dean.

The Museum of the Forest -
telling the story of this unique area.

plus

Woodland walks ≈ *Adventure playground* ≈ *Cafe*

Craft & Museum shops

Special Events (*including traditional Charcoal Burns twice a year*)

Forester's Cottage ≈ *Sculptures* ≈ *Ducks, Fowls & Dotty the Pig*

Open

Daily:
Feb & Mar 10 am - 5 pm
April - Oct 10 am - 6 pm

Weekends only:
Nov - Jan 10 am - 4 pm

Pre-booked groups welcome all year

Tel. 01594 822170

Set in a beautiful location at Soudley on the B4227 between
Cinderford & Blakeney.
Only 20 minutes from the Speech House.

A charity safeguarding the heritage and culture of the Forest of Dean.
Charity No. 298647

Tourist Attractions

National Birds of Prey Falconry Centre
Newent. Tel: (0531) 820286

Jubilee Maze
Symonds Yat West. Tel: (0600) 890360

Puzzle Wood, Perrygrove Road,
Coleford. Tel: (0594) 833187

Dean Forest Railway, Norchard,
Lydney. Tel: (0594) 843423

The World Of Butterflies, Whitchurch,
Oxenhall,Symonds Yat West.
Tel: (0600) 890471

Littledean Hall,
Littledean. Tel (0594) 824213

Goodrich Castle
Goodrich. Tel: (0600) 890538

Tintern Parva Vineyard
overlooking Tintern Abbey. Tel: (0291) 689636

Wye Valley Farm Park, Goodrich,
Ross On Wye. Tel: (0600) 890296

Clearwell Caves
Coleford. Tel: (0594) 832535

Three Choirs Vineyard,
Newent. Tel: (0531) 890223

St. Anne's Vineyard, Wane House,
Newent. Tel: (0989) 313

Caldicot Castle & Country Park
Caldicot. Tel: (0291) 420241

National Trust - Regional Info Office
Tewkesbury. Tel: (0684) 850051

Beechenhurst is the starting point for following the famous Sculpture Trail, exploring the Forest through Russells Inclosure or discovering the Forest Nature Reserve.

The site provides the perfect setting for outdoor eating - picnic tables and barbecue hearths are provided. There are open spaces where youngsters can play and an adventure playground for the under sixes.

The lodge is open throughout the year for refreshments (W.C's). During the winter months the log fire provides a special warm welcome.

Souvenirs and other forest related items are for sale in the well stocked shop. Trail leaflets, maps, guides, and information from the rangers may be obtained here before you set off to explore the Forest.

Built in timber and using local Cannop Valley stone. Beechenhurst Lodge is a good example of how good wood can be used in modern buildings.

Beechenhurst Lodge

Speechouse Hill Nr. Coleford Glos. GL16 7EJ. Tel: 0594 827357